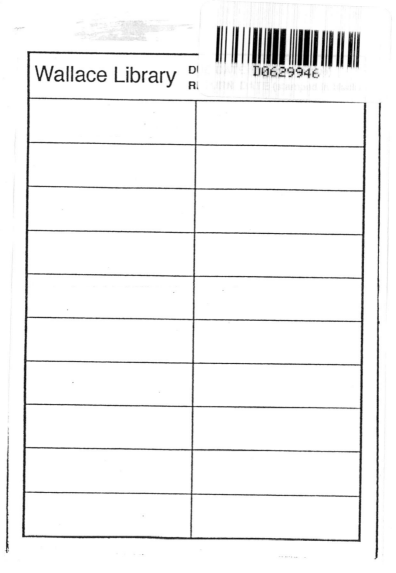

A SHORT HISTORY OF
Wisconsin

LARRY GARA

THE STATE HISTORICAL SOCIETY OF WISCONSIN

MADISON

F
581
G33

ACKNOWLEDGMENT—

The Extension Division of the University of Wisconsin co-operated
in the planning, and financially supported the writing, of this book.

**Printed in the United States of America by
Kingsport Press, Inc., Kingsport, Tennessee.**

for
ROBIN

Contents

Preface

This short history of Wisconsin was originally intended as a basic introduction to the subject for use in a correspondence course offered by the Extension Division of the state university. As such it should be used along with James I. Clark's sixteen pamphlet series, *The Chronicles of Wisconsin,* plus as much collateral reading in the sources or in scholarly monographs as might be available. The work is not intended to be a comprehensive history of Wisconsin, but rather a brief survey of the highlights presented in compact and readable form.

Similarly, the suggested further readings at the end of each chapter are only to lead the reader to some specific useful information. The list is merely a starting point and does not include all of the works consulted for writing the book. For example, a number of very useful unpublished doctoral dissertations and master's theses in the Library of the University of Wisconsin provided much valuable information and insight, but such titles were not included in the references because they are not readily available to most students or other readers. Serious students of Wisconsin history should make use of Leroy Schlinkert's *Sub-*

ject Bibliography of Wisconsin History (Madison, 1947) and peruse the wealth of source material and secondary writings in the files of the *Wisconsin Magazine of History,* the various volumes of the *Collections,* and the *Proceedings* of the State Historical Society of Wisconsin.

Working on this book has made me painfully aware of the many gaps in our knowledge of Wisconsin history, especially in the period since the Civil War. Much has been written, but there is a pressing need for a comprehensive, multi-volume history of the state. Without such a scholarly set all students of the subject must continue to work with material which is largely tentative in nature.

LARRY GARA

Spring, 1962
Grove City, Pennsylvania

CHAPTER 1

The Fur Trade Era in Wisconsin

T HE recorded history of Wisconsin begins with the arrival in 1634 of Jean Nicolet, the first European known to have visited the region. For more than a century after, Wisconsin was a frontier province of New France which had its political center in Canada. The land of Wisconsin became a pawn in the lengthy power struggle for world leadership between France and England, a struggle which had culminated by 1763 in final British victory.

British title to Wisconsin lasted only until the end of the American Revolutionary War, but British occupancy continued until 1796. However, it was not until the end of America's second war with Great Britain that the destiny of the region was fixed as a part of the total development of the United States, rather than a province of Europe. Until the final settlement of the Treaty of Ghent in 1814,

1

the trade in furs and peltry supplied the main thread of Wisconsin history.

When the French arrived they found northern Wisconsin to be a land of numerous lakes and streams and great forests of pine with some mixed hardwoods. The southern portion was partly prairie in the east and a country of deeply eroded gullies and high ridges in the western or driftless area, untouched by the great glacier which appeared about 25,000 years ago. Parts of the Wisconsin glacier advanced and receded across much of the present state for more than 15,000 years. The last glacier to cover most of Wisconsin carried soil from distant places, destroyed vegetation, crushed native rocks into soil, transformed the high ridges of old, weathered mountains into hilly slopes, and left lakes, ponds, and swamplands in its wake. The hills provided good drainage and the mixture of soils was to prove excellent for crops, but the French in Wisconsin did nothing to exploit the agricultural resources of the region.

In the colonial period the land and its geographic position lent peculiar significance to Wisconsin. It was the lakes and rivers bordering and crisscrossing Wisconsin that made it a key highway for Indians, fur traders, missionaries, and settlers. Fronting on Lakes Superior and Michigan on the north and east and bounded by the Mississippi River on the west, Wisconsin with its navigable rivers provided a natural waterway for travel to the west and the south. The Fox and Wisconsin river path with a short, easy portage became a main-traveled route from Canada through the Great Lakes to the Mississippi. For the French, and the Indians before them, this system of water highways proved to be a valuable asset. A major link in the system gave the state its name. The French called it the Ouisconsin, and the British the Wisconsin.

Wisconsin's first human inhabitants used other natural

Portaging a canoe
SHSW Colls.

resources besides the lakes and rivers. At least five distinct
Indian peoples lived in Wisconsin before the Europeans
arrived. In primitive fashion the Indians farmed its rich,
productive soil, fished in the numerous lakes and rivers,
mined its copper and lead, and hunted the birds and animals which frequented its woods and streams. Although
these people had widely different ways of life, all of them
found adequate resources for their needs in the region
which they made their home. Some of them found time to
dot the area with the symbolic effigy mounds which later
puzzled students of Indian life.

Representatives of three major Indian language groups
lived in Wisconsin when it was a European colonial province. The great majority were Algonquian who included
the Chippewa, Ottawa, Potawatomi, Mascoutin, Kickapoo, Sauk, Fox and Menominee. The Sioux in northwestern Wisconsin were gradually being driven westward by
the Chippewa; their kinsmen, the Winnebago, were found
first in northeastern Wisconsin but were pushed south-
westward. During the course of the French regime the
Iroquoian Hurons (as well as the Ottawa) also moved in
from the East.

A JESUIT DESCRIPTION OF THE WISCONSIN INDIANS

The Jesuit Fathers wrote excellent descriptions of early Wisconsin Indians. The following comment by Father Allouez describes the difficulties the Indians faced during the winter of 1669–1670. The Indians were Sauk, Potawatomi, Fox, and Winnebago at Father Allouez' mission located on the Oconto River, on or near the site of the present-day city of Oconto.

The savages of this region are more than usually barbarous; they are without ingenuity, and do not know how to make even a bark dish or a ladle; they commonly use shells. They are grasping and avaricious to an extraordinary degree, and sell their little commodities at a high price, because they have only what is barely necessary. The season in which we arrived among them was not favorable for us; they were all in a needy condition, and very little able to give us any assistance, so that we suffered hunger. But blessed be God, who gives us all these opportunities and richly recompenses, besides, all these hardships by the consolation that He makes us find, amid the greatest afflictions, in the quest of so many poor savages' souls, which are not less the work of His hands and the price of the blood of Jesus Christ, His Son, than those of the princes and sovereigns of the earth.— LOUISE PHELPS KELLOGG, ED., *Early Narratives of the Northwest, 1634–1699* (*Original Narratives of Early American History,* edited by J. F. Jameson, New York, 1917), 146.

With the arrival of the Europeans, Indian life underwent sudden and thorough changes. Previously trade had played a subordinate role in tribal relations; it soon became a primary interest. The French wanted furs and the Indians came to depend upon the products they traded for them. Wisconsin Indians set aside their chipped stone implements for iron axes and knives brought in by the French traders. European-manufactured metal kettles replaced bulky earthenware or wooden cooking pots. The Indians acquired a taste for French wines and brandies as well as a preference for European cloth and imported, brightly-colored blankets. And they quickly saw the advantages of muskets for hunting and war. In time the Indians lost many of the skills inherent in their traditional

---

THE INDIAN ATTITUDE TOWARDS THE BEAVER

The Indians quickly learned how valuable the fur trade could be to them, although they failed to realize that it would eventually make them almost wholly dependent on the Europeans. The following excerpt from the JESUIT RELATIONS, *written by Father Paul Le Jeune in 1634, illustrates how the Indians reacted to the new economic situation:*

The Castor or Beaver is taken in several ways. The Savages say that it is the animal well-beloved by the French, English and Basques,—in a word, by the Europeans. I heard my host say one day, jokingly, *Missi picoutau amiscou*, "The Beaver does everything perfectly well, it makes Kettles, hatchets, swords, knives, bread; and in short, it makes everything." He was making sport of us Europeans, who have such a fondness for the skin of this animal and who fight to see who will give the most to these Barbarians, to get it; they carry this to such an extent that my host said to me one day, showing me a very beautiful knife, "The English have no sense; they give us twenty knives like this for one Beaver skin."— *The Jesuit Relations and Allied Documents,* Selected and edited by Edna Kenton (New York, 1954), 65.

Indians hunting beaver
SHSW Colls.

past. Eventually many of them became completely dependent on the Europeans. The European's diseases, too, affected Indian life. Smallpox was especially serious; at times entire villages fell victim to sudden epidemics of the fatal disease.

Contact with the white men also set the Indians against one another in numerous trade wars, for there was no unity in the Indian world. The vast region of Wisconsin became a place of refuge during the extensive wars and migrations of the seventeenth and eighteenth centuries. The eastern Iroquois succeeded in organizing a temporary wartime confederacy of their Five Nations, and in the early seventeenth century they undertook a series of military campaigns in an attempt to break the fur trade monopoly of the Hurons. As a result the Hurons moved into Wisconsin and caused the Indians already there to shift about. The Winnebago, who fought the Hurons, the Iroquois, the Illinois, and the Chippewa, were finally driven southward. The Ottawa also fought the Iroquois and moved into Wisconsin from the northeast. Neither the Ottawa nor the Hurons remained in Wisconsin more than a dozen years. The Potawatomi of eastern Wisconsin moved south and then migrated into Ohio, as did the Kickapoo. The Mascoutin of the upper Fox River valley were partly absorbed by the Fox; others moved south into Illinois. The Sauk and Fox, who consistently fought the French, eventually migrated to Iowa. Only the Menominee near the Menominee River and in the Fox River valley did not move about.

In the frequent clashes between English and French, the Iroquois usually sided with the British with whom they traded, while their enemies and blood relatives, the Hurons, sided and traded with the French. However, Indian alliances shifted and various tribes would sometimes ally with the French and at other times with the British. No Indian leader succeeded in uniting all the Indians against the Europeans. The Indian world lacked both the concept of unity and the necessary governmental machinery for such an effort.

For more than fifty years the Fox Indians carried on desperate warfare with the French but they could not rely upon their Indian allies. In the early eighteenth century Kiala, a Fox chief from Wisconsin, attempted to build up an anti-French coalition including tribes as remote as the Abenaki in the East and the Sioux of the West. The coalition collapsed when the Sioux defected. In the summer of 1733 the Fox accepted defeat and surrendered at La Baye (Green Bay). The French sold Chief Kiala into West Indian slavery and chased the remnant of the Fox into Iowa.

The Europeans made good use of inter-tribal rivalry for their own purposes. The Indians, after all, played a vital role in the fur trade, and in all their dealings in the New World the French officials were always conscious of that trade. It made Wisconsin one of their valuable holdings and attracted the jealous attention of the British to the north and the east. Woods surrounded Wisconsin's rivers and lakes, and the forests swarmed with fur-bearing ani-

---

---

mals. Deer, elk, marten, lynx, bear, and above all, beaver lived in the region. The French failed to find new supplies of precious metals as the Spanish had located in their colonies, but they came upon an abundance of furs at the very time when beaver hats were all the rage in Europe, and high officials of church and state wore magnificent fur coats. Paris was the center of the European trade, but merchants shipped furs and fur products to places as far

---

---

away as Russia. The international fur trade played an important part in commerce and contributed to French national development in an era when each European ruler hoped to make his nation supreme by exporting more goods than it imported.

French fur traders home from the woods
SHSW Colls.

At first the fur trade was a simple affair. A *bourgeois* or owner of a canoe and trading outfit purchased the necessary goods and supplies and hired six or seven *voyageurs* who navigated and paddled the bulky canoe, carried the supplies when it was necessary to travel overland to reach another water route, repaired the canoe, and provided the manual labor needed on the journey. Some *voyageurs* contracted for a single short trip while others agreed to work in the woods for a year or longer. The entire trade rested on a system of credit which the Montreal merchants used to purchase European goods and the *bourgeois* used to hire his *voyageurs*. Some traders gave goods in advance to the Indians in order to win their friendship and their business.

It was the fur trade that first attracted the French to Wisconsin. In 1634 Jean Nicolet left Lake Huron for parts unknown, his mission to make peace among the Indians and to seal an alliance with them. Robed in a colorful garment of China damask and carrying a pistol in each hand Nicolet landed in the Green Bay area. He succeeded in making a pact with the Winnebago and other nearby

Landing of Nicolet near Green Bay

JEAN NICOLET'S MEETING WITH THE WINNEBAGOS, 1634

Father Charles Raymbault, a good friend of Jean Nicolet, wrote the following description of Nicolet's journey:

He embarked in the Huron country, with seven savages; and they passed by many small nations, both going and returning. When they arrived at their destination, they fastened two sticks in the earth, and hung gifts thereon, so as to relieve these tribes from the notion of mistaking them for enemies to be massacred. When he was two days' journey from that nation, he sent one of those savages to bear tidings of the peace, which word was especially well received when they heard that it was a European who carried the message; they despatched several young men to meet the Manitouiriniou—that is to say, "the wonderful man." They meet him; they escort him, and carry all his baggage. He wore a grand robe of China damask, all strewn with flowers and birds of many colors. No sooner did they perceive him than the women and children fled, at the sight of a man who carried thunder in both hands—for thus they called the two pistols that he held. The news of his coming quickly spread to the places round about, and there assembled four or five thousand men. Each of the chief men made a feast for him, and at one of these banquets they served at least sixscore beavers. The peace was concluded; he returned to the Hurons, and some time later to the Three Rivers, where he continued his employment as agent and interpreter, to the great satisfaction of both the French and the savages, by whom he was equally and singularly loved.—KELLOGG, *Early Narratives*, 16.

Indians, and he opened new areas for the French fur trade. Two decades later Medart Chouart Sieur de Grosseilliers and a French companion led a trading expedition into the Green Bay area. In 1659, without the permission of French officials, he returned with his brother-in-law, Pierre Esprit Radisson. On this trip Radisson and Grosseilliers constructed a building for the fur trade supplies on the shores of Chequamegon Bay, visited and talked with the Ottawa at the village in Lac Court Oreilles (in present-day Sawyer County), and held a great council with the Indians at Superior. After three years in the Wisconsin forests, the two traders returned to Canada with sixty canoes loaded with furs. The French governor confiscated the furs because the traders were not licensed, but their voyage helped establish the Ottawa as the middlemen for the Wisconsin fur trade. Other French traders visited the Ottawa in the Lake Superior area periodically until 1667 when a temporary Iroquois peace treaty made it possible to shift the center of the Wisconsin trade to Green Bay.

At Green Bay the Potawatomi replaced the Ottawa as the middlemen of the French trade. The trading arrangement was worked out by Nicolas Perrot who lived in the west as a trader and explorer from 1667 to 1698. Perrot,

---

PERROT'S ARRIVAL AT THE INDIAN VILLAGE NEAR BERLIN

The arrival of the Frenchmen was the occasion for a series of festivities described in the following account:
The great chief of the Miamis came to meet them, at the head of more than three thousand men, accompanied by the chiefs of other tribes who formed part of the village. Each of these chiefs had a calumet, . . . they were entirely naked, wearing only shoes, which were artistically embroidered like buskins; they sang, as they approached, the calumet song, which they uttered in cadence. When they reached the Frenchmen, they continued their songs, meanwhile bending their knees, in

turn, almost to the ground. They presented the calumet to the sun, with the same genuflexions, and then they came back to the principal Frenchman, with many gesticulations. Some played upon instruments the calumet songs, and others sang them, holding the calumet to the mouth without lighting it. A war chief raised Perrot upon his shoulders, and, accompanied by all the musicians, conducted him to the village. The Maskoutech who had been his guide offered him to the Miamis, to be lodged among them; they very amiably declined, being unwilling to deprive the Maskoutechs of the pleasure of possessing a Frenchman who had consented to come under their auspices. At last he was taken to the cabin of the chief of the Maskoutechs; as he entered, the lighted calumet was presented to him, which he smoked; and fifty guardsmen were provided for him, who prevented the crowd from annoying him. A grand repast was served, the various courses of which reminded one of feeding-troughs rather than dishes; the food was seasoned with the fat of the wild ox [buffalo]. The guards took good care that provisions should be brought often, for they profited thereby.—"Adventures of Nicolas Perrot," by La Potherie, 1665–1670, in KELLOGG, *Early Narratives*, 85–86.

a highly skilled Indian trader, had considerable influence with the Indians around Fox River and extended the trade into that part of Wisconsin. His important work paved the way for French control of the Northwest. When new Iroquois wars broke out in 1680 Perrot succeeded in keeping some of the Wisconsin tribes loyal to the French and even led a group of Winnebago, Sauk, Fox and Menominee eastward to fight them.

Nicolas Perrot was but one of many leaders of New France who became involved in the Wisconsin fur trade. Very few farmers or *habitants* settled in the region during

After arriving at the village near the present site of Berlin, on the upper Fox River, Nicolas Perrot presented his hosts with gifts of a gun and a kettle and made the following speech:

"Men, I admire your youths; although they have since their birth seen only shadows, they seem to me as fine-looking as those who are born in regions where the sun always displays his glory. I would not have believed that the earth, the mother of all men, could have furnished you the means of subsistence when you did not possess the light of the Frenchman, who supplies its influences to many peoples; I believe that you will become another nation when you become acquainted with him. I am the dawn of that light, which is beginning to appear in your lands, as it were, that which precedes the sun, who will soon shine brightly and will cause you to be born again, as if in another land, where you will find, more easily and in greater abundance, all that can be necessary to man. I see this fine village filled with young men, who are, I am sure, as courageous as they are well built; and who will, without doubt, not fear their enemies if they carry French weapons. It is for these young men that I leave my gun, which they must regard as the pledge of my esteem for their valor; they must use it if they are attacked. It will also be more satisfactory in hunting cattle and other animals than are all the arrows that you use. To you who are old men I leave my kettle; I carry it everywhere without fear of breaking it. You will cook in it the meat that your young men bring from the chase, and the food which you offer to the Frenchmen who come to visit you."

He tossed a dozen awls and knives to the women, and said to them: "Throw aside your bone bodkins; these French awls will be much easier to use. These knives will be more useful to you in killing beavers and in cutting

your meat than are the pieces of stone that you use."
Then, throwing to them some rassade [round beads of
glass or porcelain]: "See; these will better adorn your
children and girls than do their usual ornaments." The
Miamis said, by way of excuse for not having any beaver-
skins, that they had until then roasted those animals.—
"Adventures of Nicolas Perrot," in KELLOGG, *Early Narratives*, 86–87.

the French regime as they did in the Illinois country to
the south. A harsh climate, the long-drawn-out Fox wars
of the early eighteenth century and the presence of numerous varieties of fur-bearing animals in Wisconsin all
contributed to an emphasis on trade rather than settlement. The adventuresome Daniel Greysolon, Sieur Duluth, traveled through northern Wisconsin and other parts
of the West from 1678 to 1689, negotiating Indian treaties
and opening new areas to the traders. Robert Cavalier,
Sieur de La Salle, planned to establish a great French
colonial empire in the New World, with centers in the
northern and southern ends of the Mississippi River, and
with the fur trade as an economic basis. He also wanted to
expand the trade using improved and larger ships to replace the canoes of the *voyageurs*. His sailing vessel the

THE FUR TRADERS AS EXPLORERS

*All attempts of the French authorities to centralize or
control the fur trade ended in failure. The traders went
into the woods and made contact with numerous Indian
peoples. In the process they also observed lands remote
from Montreal. In 1697 Aubert de la Chesnaye reported
in a memoir:*

At first the French went only among the Hurons, and
since then to Missilimakinak, where they sold their goods

to the savages of the places, who in turn went to exchange them with other savages in the depths of the woods, lands and rivers. But at present the French, having licenses, in order to secure greater profit surreptitiously, pass all the Ottawas and savages of Missilimakinak in order to go themselves to seek the most distant tribes, which is very displeasing to the former. *It is they, also, who have made excellent discoveries;* and four or five hundred young men, the best men of Canada, are engaged in this business. . . . They have given us knowledge of many names of savages that we did not know; and four or five hundred leagues more remote are others who are unknown to us.—Frederick Jackson Turner, "The Character and Influence of the Indian Trade in Wisconsin," in MOOD, *Early Writings of Turner*, 113–114.

Griffon was the first on the Great Lakes. It left Green Bay with a full cargo of furs in 1679 but never reached its destination. Although La Salle's empire never came into being, his claiming the lower Mississippi Valley for France made possible the founding of New Orleans, which soon became an important fur trading station and export center.

Even the missionaries became involved in the fur trade. The French people in America were devout Catholics, and Jesuit and Recollect missionaries served them and entered the Wisconsin forests along with the traders. After the decline of Spanish power, France inherited the role of Europe's most powerful Catholic nation, and its government, for reasons both spiritual and material, encouraged these laborers for God in the New World. They worked alongside the fur traders and accompanied them on trips of exploration.

Wisconsin's first missionary was Father Rene Ménard, a fifty-six-year-old Jesuit of poor health but great spiritual strength. Father Ménard left Quebec in 1660 to establish

To the Jesuit missionaries of New France the Indians of America were potential converts to the faith. The following excerpt from the JESUIT RELATION *of 1660, written by Father Jerome Lalemant, tells of the opportunities and some of the difficulties in converting the natives.*

The Ocean which separates us from France sees on its eastern side, only rejoicing, splendor, and bonfires; but on its western, nothing but war, slaughter, and conflagrations.

What consoles us is our full assurance that people do not regard us merely as do those who, being themselves in port or on shore, contemplate with compassion the wreck of a poor vessel shattered by the storm, and even shed some tears over it. But we promise ourselves much more, knowing the prayers, and all sorts of good works which are being performed for the conversion of our Savages; and learning of the good purposes with which God has inspired many persons of merit, for accomplishing the destruction of the Iroquois.

That means to open a door, high and wide, for proclaiming the Faith and giving the Preachers of the Gospel access to people of great extent, in regard to both the territories which they occupy, and the diversity of nations composing them—all of whom are four or five hundred leagues distant from us in the forests, shunning the common enemy. Were it not for the latter, they would come and enrich this country with their furs, and we should visit them and enrich Heaven with the glorious spoils that we should wrest from the powers of Hell.

We know—and we will state the facts more fully—that there are tribes of the same language, both stationary and wandering, as far as the North sea, on whose shores these nations border; and that there are others, very recently discovered, extending as far as the South sea. They stretch out their arms to us, and we ours to

> them, but on both sides they are too short to unite across such a distance; and when, finally, we are on the point of embracing each other, the Iroquois steps in between and showers blows upon both of us.—KENTON, *Jesuit Relations*, 302.

missions among the Ottawa Indians, who earlier had been in contact with Christian missionaries in western Ontario. Chosen because of his expert knowledge of the Indians and their language, Ménard accepted his assignment cheerfully, even though he realized it would probably

Silver Ostensorium presented by Nicolas Perrot to the Jesuit Mission of St. Francis Xavier at De Pere, 1686.
On display at the Neville Public Museum, Green Bay.

lead to his death. His difficult trip was made worse by abusive Indian guides who stinted on his rations and forced the aging priest to carry heavy loads of supplies over frequent portages. At the small Ottawa camp he faced an insolent chief who forced him to build his own crude hut for a winter shelter. In the spring Father Ménard and several fur traders pushed on to the main Ottawa village on Lake Superior. There he learned that a group of Hurons along the Black River faced starvation because the hostile Iroquois surrounded them and refused to permit them to hunt. Father Ménard decided to visit the besieged Hurons and baptize them before they perished. The traders could not dissuade him. "God calls me thither and I must go," he said, "although it should cost me my life." He set out with some guides and traders, all but one of whom abandoned him. At one point he stepped out of the canoe to lighten its load at a place of rough rapids. The canoeman tried in vain to find the courageous priest, but Father Ménard was never seen again.

Other pioneering priests followed through on Father Ménard's sacrificial efforts. Father Claude Allouez, who worked among the Indians from 1665 until his death in 1689, was considerably more successful than his predecessor, Father Ménard. After a very difficult trip from Montreal, Father Allouez reached the Ottawa Indian villages at La Pointe du St. Esprit, on the western tip of Lake Superior, and re-established the missionary activities which Father Ménard had begun. Father Allouez brought Christian teaching to a number of western Indians, including the Huron and Sioux who lived west of Lake Superior. In 1669 Allouez traveled to the Potawatomi village on Green Bay and established new missions in the Fox River area, including St. Francis Xavier, at the site of present-day De Pere, which became the focal point for Jesuit activity in the area.

After 1675 Father Allouez left the Wisconsin area, first to continue the work begun by Father Jacques Marquette with the Illinois Indians to the south, and later to minister to the Miami of southern Michigan. His contacts with numerous Indian peoples enabled Father Allouez to make valuable observations on their manner of living. He baptized and instructed thousands during his years in Wisconsin and the West. Another Jesuit reported: "We would need here almost as much time for following Father Claude Allouez in an account of his apostolic journeys, as

---

FATHER ALLOUEZ' JOURNEY INTO WISCONSIN, 1669–1670

In a letter to his Father Superior, Father Allouez described some of the hardships involved in his trip to Wisconsin.

On the fourteenth, God delivered us from two great dangers, through the intercession of our protectors. While we were taking a little rest, our canoe was borne away from us by a gust of wind, which carried it to the other side of the river; then it was brought back to us by another gust of wind, when, awakened by the noise it made, we were thinking of making a raft, in order to go and get it. Toward evening, after making a long day's journey and finding no place for disembarking, by reason of the inaccessible banks, we were forced to remain out in the stream during the night; but, being surprised by an unusual gust of wind, we were obliged to land among rocks, where our canoe would have been shattered if God in His Providence had not taken charge of our guidance. In this second danger we appealed to Him by the mediation of our intercessors, and afterward said mass in thanksgiving.—Letter from Father Allouez to His Reverend Father Superior in 1670, in KELLOGG, *Early Narratives of the Northwest*, 144–145.

---

he took in making them; for he has not visited a single Nation without performing deeds for the glory of God, that would be very long to relate."

The Jesuit fathers continued to work along with the fur traders but their interests sometimes conflicted. The Jesuits favored a policy of restricting the influence of the traders as much as possible and keeping a close eye on their activities. In 1698 the French monarch, Louis XIV, responded to Jesuit pressure and forbade the traders to enter Indian country. The Indians were to carry their furs to certain French posts instead. By the time of Louis XIV's death in 1715 the policy had clearly failed, and a system of licensing fur traders was substituted for it.

Because of widespread Jesuit influence at the French court and their influence on New World governmental policy, the Jesuits played another role in early Wisconsin history. The priests were French as well as Catholic, and they participated in most official events in French North America. Father Allouez took part in the ceremony at Sault St. Marie in June, 1671, when France officially annexed all of North America in the presence of representatives of more than a dozen Indian tribes. Father Jacques Marquette, a skilled map maker and scholar of Indian tongues, accompanied the Louis Jolliet expedition of 1673, which was probably the first to travel much of the length of the Mississippi River. The presence of priests with traders, French military forces, and exploratory parties lent support to the claim that France represented Christian truth as well as political power. Missionary activity gradually declined in the face of continued failure to convert the Indians. The most lasting contributions of the Jesuit fathers were not what they had hoped for. Rather than great numbers of Christian converts, the priests left detailed and accurate descriptions of the land,

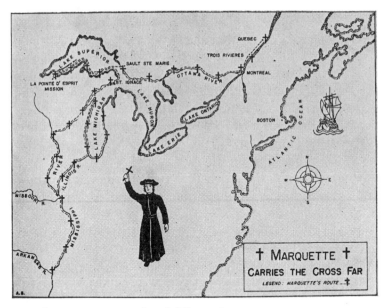

French missionaries explored Wisconsin
SHSW Colls.

sympathetic accounts of the Indian inhabitants, and scholarly studies of the various Indian languages.

Just as they had failed to Christianize the Indians, the priests had little success in their efforts to promote the idea of a centrally-controlled fur trade. The fur trade of Wisconsin and the West, by its very nature, defied regulation by the authorities of New France. The traders consistently ignored French laws and regulations which conflicted with their interests. In 1717, at the end of the first Fox war, Louis de la Porte de Louvigny, the French military commander, forbade traders to visit the Fox villages but sadly admitted that "prohibitions of this sort have not been very well enforced." The great majority of fur traders were *couriers de bois*, illegal, unlicensed traders as distinct from those who accepted a modicum of control over their trading pursuits. One French official estimated that of ten thousand inhabitants in New France, eight hundred men had gone into the woods as illegal traders. These individualists of the woods could make bargains on their own terms. They often lived with Indian women. They sold their furs and pelts wherever they could get the most for them, sometimes at stipulated trading posts, sometimes in Louisiana to the south, and not infrequently to the British merchants in the East who often paid better prices than the French.

Meanwhile, both French and British colonials maneuvered for position in their competition for the Indian trade. Charles de Langlade, the son of a French fur trader and his Ottawa Indian wife, played a significant role in the rivalry. The Langlades moved to Green Bay from Mackinac just before Charles took up arms in the French cause. He was devoutly loyal and especially interested in keeping Wisconsin's fur trade in French hands. In 1724 British-American merchants had established a trading post at Oswego, New York. Other traders, backed by merchants from Pennsylvania and Virginia, entered the Ohio valley and the region south of the Great Lakes. In 1748 the British-Americans built a post named Pickawillany (Piqua, Ohio) on the Big Miami River. Despite the eight hundred miles to Philadelphia, large numbers of Indian traders transported goods to the post and for four years the Pickawillany merchants carried on a profitable business. George Croghan, a skilled trader and Indian scout, by shrewd negotiating won the friendship of a number of the Miami tribes whom he alienated from the French.

When officials of New France became alarmed over developments in the Ohio valley they chose Wisconsin's Charles de Langlade to lead an Indian force against the Pickawillany post. His Indian followers from the Mackinac area attacked the fort, captured the British there, and killed fourteen of the Miami and Shawnee Indians who had helped defend it. In a cannibalistic rite the victorious fought against France, Russia, and Austria. A series of defeats from Canada to India brought a sudden end to the French colonial empire. In 1763, with the signing of the Treaty of Paris, France ceded all of Canada and her lands east of the Mississippi River to the British. At the same time Spain secured title to the vast Louisiana Territory stretching west from the Mississippi to the Rockies.

To the British, as to the French, Wisconsin continued to have significance mainly because of the fur trade. Except for the Indians and the traders, it was still a largely unsettled wilderness. The British stationed no governmental officials in Wisconsin; there was no civil government. During the French and Indian War they established one military post at Green Bay and for nearly two years after October, 1761, Lieutenant James Gorrell commanded the small garrison. He rebuilt the fort and named it Fort Edward Augustus. It was primarily a trading center, and Gorrell's major task was to quiet the Indians who longed for a return of French rule and who were quick to believe rumors of such a development.

In 1763 what began as an Indian alliance to oust the British from Detroit developed into more serious Indian troubles under the leadership of the Ottawa chief, Pontiac. In Wisconsin the only direct result of the general Indian uprising was the murder of two traders at English Prairie (Muscoda). The Sauk, Fox, Winnebago and Menominee of Wisconsin did not join Pontiac, but Gorrell and his men left Green Bay in June, 1763, to rescue some Indian captives. After that date no British military forces were stationed in Wisconsin.

Shortly afterwards, the British government drew a line along the crest of the Allegheny Mountains and forbade settlers to enter territory west of the line. The Proclamation Line was a temporary expedient to regulate Indian affairs and prevent outbursts like the one led by Pontiac.

Indians ate Old Briton, the chief of the pro-British Miamis. Langlade's victory temporarily thwarted the British threat to the western fur trade and put the Northwest once again under French control. The fight at Pickawillany was the first incident in the French and Indian War, the last of four Anglo-French conflicts which were fought in part in America. Langlade served under the French flag throughout the conflict and helped bring Wisconsin Indians into the field of battle. He took some Indians eastward to help defend Fort Duquesne, and it was Langlade who advised attacking the British General Edward Braddock before he reached the fort. With more Wisconsin Indians he later fought under Marquis de Montcalm on the Plains of Abraham in defense of Quebec, and also at the subsequent battle of Ste. Foy.

Although the French and Indian War began in America, it soon merged into the Seven Years' War which broke out in Europe in 1756. England and her ally Prussia

Braddock's defeat near Fort Duquesne

For a while at least the western region was to be Indian country traversed only by traders or soldiers sent out to regulate the trade. Meanwhile British officials made plans and negotiated some Indian treaties for the orderly and peaceful settlement of the West. But Parliament reversed this policy with the Quebec Act of 1774, which placed the whole of the Northwest between the Ohio and the Mississippi in the colony of Quebec, and forbade further settlement by the British-Americans. The outbreak of war between the American colonies and England prevented the Quebec Act from going into effect.

Under the British, changes took place in the direction and control of the fur trade. Montreal continued to be the American center of the trade, but the furs now went to London instead of Paris. English investors replaced the French capitalists, and the traders used more English manufactured goods than they had previously. French and Spanish traders, operating from St. Louis, competed with the British for the furs in the Illinois country, along the Wabash River, and even in Wisconsin. A number of rival British traders and trading firms combined to form larger companies and eventually a few giant concerns carried on the bulk of the trade, dividing the fur-bearing country among themselves. Traders also penetrated the far Northwest to the Pacific after keen competition and the partial depletion of the beaver supply in Wisconsin and the neighboring region made such expansion necessary. The long route west required several years and considerably more investment capital for larger consignments of goods and bigger boats to transport them. Powerful merchants also demanded more strict control over their workers and traders when involved in the distant trade. All of these factors further encouraged the growth of large trading companies.

In the forests of Wisconsin, however, there was very

little change with the coming of the British regime. Most of the *voyageurs* were still the same French-Canadians who had been hard at work before the arrival of the British. English traders learned what they knew from the French and continued to hire them for the trade in the woods. The Indians preferred dealing with the French, whom they knew and with whom they were often related. As before, the trader's life was a free one. Regulation of the trade proved as difficult under the British as it had under the French. The independent life of the trader attracted some fugitives and criminals, and the disreputable element frequently contributed to Indian troubles.

Even the early years of the American Revolution had little noticeable effect on the Wisconsin fur trade. During the first phase of the war the British controlled the entire Northwest and the traders went about their business without interruption. But things changed rapidly after George Rogers Clark, acting under authorization from Virginia, carried the war westward with his invasion of the Illinois country in 1778. From then until the close of the conflict most fur trading in Wisconsin and the land south of the Great Lakes ceased, although traders continued large-scale activity in the area to the north and west of Lake Superior.

Both Indians and traders participated in the Revolutionary War. The Wisconsin Indians and French-Canadian *voyageurs* tended to sympathize more with the Americans than the British. Yet the latter gained half-hearted support from both groups at various times by promising trade and distributing much needed goods and supplies. Traders often sold their manufactured items to the British military officers for high prices, and the British gave the goods to the Indians in return for military service. The Indian market for such goods was endless, and after every raid on a western settlement the red men demanded more. By the use of such "trinket diplomacy" the upper part of the Northwest, including Wisconsin, remained nominally British until the end of the war.

After the Revolution there was little immediate change in Wisconsin. The handful of French settlers lived much as they had before. The fur trade continued to dominate economic life. Technically the region was American, but actually the British continued to control the fur trade from the various posts they had established earlier. The Wisconsin trade centered around Mackinac, outside the present borders of the state. The Treaty of Paris of 1783 provided that these posts should be turned over to the Americans "with all convenient speed," but the British found numerous excuses to delay the transfer. Another Anglo-American agreement, Jay's Treaty of 1794, made more definite provision for the removal of British forces from the Northwest. By 1796 all the northwestern posts were in American hands. The British, however, continued to monopolize the fur trade from the Canadian side of the border. Jay's Treaty gave British traders the same privileges as Americans and with such an advantage they dominated the American trade until after the War of 1812.

America's second war with Great Britain was also a phase of a greater European conflict. The British considered the French, whom they again began fighting in 1793, to be their chief enemy. Among the grievances which helped prepare the new American nation for war was the alleged British stirring up of the Indians against the Americans in the West. Before the United States declared war on Great Britain, William Henry Harrison, governor of Indiana Territory, had fought the Indians at the indecisive battle of Tippecanoe. Tecumseh, a Shawnee chief, and his brother, a religious leader called the Prophet, endeavored to unite all of the Indians against the oncoming white men. This time some Wisconsin Indians, conscious

John Jacob Astor, the Prince of Fur Traders
SHSW Colls.

of their eventual fate should westward expansion continue, took active part in the Indian wars. Winnebago
from Wisconsin fought at the battle of Tippecanoe and
also at the battle of the Thames in 1813, where the Americans defeated the combined Indian forces and killed Tecumseh. Robert Dickson, a red-haired Scotsman and Indian trader, organized some of the Wisconsin Indians and
fur traders for the British cause.

Frontier fur trading post
Photograph of a SHSW diorama

During the early part of the War of 1812 the British took the posts at Detroit, Mackinac, and Fort Dearborn. The Northwest was in British hands during most of the war, though Americans occupied Prairie du Chien briefly. William Clark, a Superintendent for Indian Affairs stationed at St. Louis, traveled up the Mississippi with a small force in June, 1814. He built a garrison called Fort Shelby at Prairie du Chien, and for the first time an American flag flew over a building in Wisconsin. It was not there long, however, for a month later the British took the fort.

The Treaty of Ghent which ended the War of 1812 settled none of the problems over which the war had been fought, but it did restore boundaries to their prewar status. It was the last European treaty to deal directly with Wisconsin as a part of the American West, and its result was to break the British stranglehold on the fur trade and to pave the way for eventual American occupancy.

The Americans were interested in Wisconsin for more than the trade in furs. American settlers constantly sought new land. They founded villages, farmed the land, and developed small industries. A westward movement of farmer settlers headed slowly but steadily across the Ohio Valley and towards Wisconsin. The Americans saw in Wisconsin a place to live and colonize rather than just a region in which to obtain furs or trade with the Indians.

The conflict between those who favored setting aside the Northwest as an Indian buffer state supported by the fur trade, and those who wished to see the area opened to white settlement had been building up for many years. Great Britain had promoted the buffer region idea with the Proclamation Line of 1763 and the short-lived Quebec Act of 1774. At the close of the American Revolution British diplomats in Paris had tried to persuade the Americans to set up such an Indian territory, and British fur traders had promoted the plan when it came up for discussion during the negotiations preceding Jay's Treaty. Finally, at Ghent, the British demanded acceptance of a buffer region as a condition to ending the War of 1812. When the Americans refused, the British then proposed a boundary based on military possession. This, too, would have placed Wisconsin in the British Empire and probably would have relegated it to the status of an Indian territory. But eventually the British diplomats agreed to accept the prewar boundaries and on this basis the Northwest was clearly part of the United States.

Even during the British regime there were some in both England and America who did not favor setting aside the entire region for the Indians and the traders. In America, Robert Rogers, who gained fame as the leader of Rogers' Rangers during the French and Indian War, made extensive plans for establishing a colony in the interior of the Mississippi Valley. Rogers' plan included all of Wisconsin. A number of influential colonial land speculators, including Benjamin Franklin and the Philadelphia firm of Baynton, Wharton and Morgan, also envisioned settling the

Northwest with British-Americans. While he was Prime Minister, William Petty-Fitzmaurice, Lord Shelburne, favored setting up a number of interior colonies after the Indians had agreed and had gradually moved elsewhere. To Shelburne this was a natural follow-up to the temporary policy of restriction adopted in 1763. He also suggested deporting the French settlers from the Illinois country just as the Acadians had been deported earlier from Nova Scotia. But Shelburne lost power and Parliament turned to a different program with the ill-fated Quebec Act of 1774.

The writings of Jonathan Carver also popularized the idea of Wisconsin as a place for settlement. Carver was a New England soldier, explorer, map maker and draftsman who traveled through much of Wisconsin searching for a water route to the western sea. Major Robert Rogers, British commander at Mackinac, had planned the expedition of which Carver was only a subordinate member. They found no northwest passage, but Carver made careful and detailed notes of what he saw along the way. He later moved to England where in 1778 he published his *Travels through the Interior Posts of North-America, in the Years 1766, 1767, and 1768.* This first description of Wisconsin penned by an English writer quickly became a best seller, running into numerous editions in England as well as on the Continent. Many Europeans got their impressions of North America from Carver's book. He pilfered some of his material from earlier French writers, but much of it was based on his own personal observations. Stories concerning an Indian deed which granted Carver ten thousand acres of land now in Minnesota and Wisconsin circulated after his death led to a century of futile court litigation by his heirs.

Carver exaggerated his role in planning and carrying on the expedition, but he furnished a valuable, detailed ac-

JONATHAN CARVER'S EVALUATION OF THE MISSISSIPPI VALLEY

To Carver the Mississippi Valley seemed to be a natural place for settlement by Europeans, who would bring industry and commerce into the region. The following brief description summarizes his ideas on the potentialities of the American West:

The Mississippi, as I have before observed, runs from north to south, and passes through the most fertile and temperate part of North America, excluding only the extremities of it, which verge both on the torrid and frigid zones. Thus favourably situated, when once its banks are covered with inhabitants, they need not long be at a loss for means to establish an extensive and profitable commerce. They will find the country towards the south almost spontaneously producing silk, cotton, indico [sic], and tobacco; and the more northern parts, wine, oil, beef, tallow, skins, buffalo-wool, and furs; with lead, copper, iron, coals, lumber, corn, rice, and fruits, besides earth and barks for dying.

These articles, with which it abounds even to profusion, may be transported to the ocean through this river without greater difficulty than that which attends the conveyance of merchandize down some of those I have just mentioned. It is true that the Mississippi being the boundary between the English and Spanish settlements, and the Spaniards in possession of the mouth of it, they may obstruct the passage of it, and greatly dishearten those who make the first attempts; yet when the advantages that will certainly arise to settlers are known, multitudes of adventurers, allured by the prospect of such abundant riches, will flock to it, and establish themselves, though at the expense of rivers of blood.— CARVER, *Travels*, 528–529.

Captain Jonathan Carver
SHSW Colls.

count of Wisconsin, its Indian inhabitants, and its natural resources. He especially emphasized its fertile soil and called attention to its advantages for agricultural pursuits. Carver's travel account described Wisconsin as an ideal location for English settlers. It helped promote the idea that the land in the Northwest had far more potential than those interested only in the fur trade had dreamed. Jonathan Carver prophesied that in the American West of some future time "mighty kingdoms will emerge from these wildernesses, and stately palaces and solemn temples, with gilded spires reaching the skies, supplant the Indian huts, whose only decorations are the barbarous trophies of their vanquished enemies."

Carver published the first edition of his book during the American Revolution when the Northwestern country and the fur trade were still under British control. At the time no one knew that the Americans would get the land and that as a result the fur trade would gradually move out and the settlers move in. In 1816 the United States Congress passed a law excluding aliens from the American fur trade. By that year John Jacob Astor's American Fur Company had nearly monopolized the fur trade of Wisconsin. But Astor and the other fur magnates were seeking richer fields of operation in the Far West. The partial depletion of Wisconsin's animal population along with competition from government owned and operated trading posts or factories stimulated the westward movement of the fur trade. The traders continued their work in the less thickly settled parts of Wisconsin but the trade dwindled steadily in importance. In the territorial period which followed the War of 1812 Americans began to find new—and in the long run far more valuable—assets in Wisconsin.

SUGGESTED ADDITIONAL READING

Campbell, Henry Colin. *Wisconsin in Three Centuries, 1634–1905* (5 volumes, New York, 1906), vol. I, *Wisconsin as a Province*.

Carver, Jonathan. *Travels through the Interior Parts of North America, in the Years 1766, 1767, and 1768* (London, 1781; facsimile edition, Minneapolis, 1956).

Clark, James I. *Father Claude Allouez, Missionary* (Madison, 1957).

—————. *Wisconsin: Land of Frenchmen, Indians, and the Beaver* (Madison, 1955).

—————. *The British Leave Wisconsin: The War of 1812* (Madison, 1955).

Curtis, John T. *The Vegetation of Wisconsin: An Ordination of Plant Communities* (Madison, 1959).

Douglass, John M., *The Indians in Wisconsin History* (Milwaukee, 1954).

Draper, Lyman C., ed. "Augustin Grignon's Recollections," in the *Wisconsin Historical Collections*, 3:195–295.

Hunt, George T. *The Wars of the Iroquois: A Study in Intertribal Relations* (Madison, 1940).

Kellogg, Louise Phelps. *The British Regime in Wisconsin and the Northwest* (Madison, 1935).

—————. *The French Regime in Wisconsin and the Northwest* (Madison, 1925).

—————. "The First Missionary in Wisconsin," in the *Wisconsin Magazine of History*, 4:417–425 (June, 1921).

Quaife, Milo M., *Wisconsin, Its History and Its People, 1634–1924* (4 volumes, Chicago, 1924), I, 1–359.

—————. "Jonathan Carver and the Carver Grant," in the *Mississippi Valley Historical Review*, 7:3–25 (June, 1920).

—————. "An Experiment of the Fathers in State Socialism," in the *Wisconsin Magazine of History*, 3:277–290 (March, 1920).

Raney, William Francis, *Wisconsin: A Story of Progress* (New York, 1940), 1–62.

Ritzenthaler, Robert Eugene, *Prehistoric Indians of Wisconsin* (Milwaukee, 1953).

Turner, Frederick Jackson, "The Character and Influence of the Indian Trade in Wisconsin," in Fulmer Mood, ed., *The Early Writings of Frederick Jackson Turner* (Madison, 1938), 87–181.

CHAPTER 2

Wisconsin as a Frontier Territory 1814–1848

THIRTY-FOUR years after the close of the War of 1812 Wisconsin entered the union as a state. During those three and a half decades settlers had steadily entered the region and gradually transformed parts of it from a frontier wilderness to an outpost of civilization. Military rule gradually but certainly gave way to civilian government. Most of the Indian inhabitants, who had played so important a role in the earlier history, moved elsewhere. Miners, pioneer farmers, land speculators, merchants, and other frontier businessmen all contributed to Wisconsin's development. In general terms the frontier experience of Wisconsin was much the same as that of other places, but in

38

detail there were vast differences. Unique circumstances set Wisconsin's frontier history apart from that of other states.

While agricultural lands beckoned individuals to many American frontiers, it was the lead region of southwestern Wisconsin that first attracted settlers to the area. Some of the lead region's most valuable deposits lay south and west beyond the present boundaries of the state, but about five-sixths of the lead-producing district was in Wisconsin. The settlers were miners, the majority of them from the southern states, especially Kentucky and Tennessee. Some had previously worked in other frontier mining regions. There was a growing market for lead, used in the manufacture of paint and shot, and a steep rise in its price stimulated a rush in the late 1820's. The Wisconsin lead region became a new frontier and its population boomed from two hundred in 1825 to four thousand the following year and ten thousand a few years later.

Prior to 1847 the government leased, rather than sold, the mineral lands but the policy encouraged fraud. Many mineral tracts were purchased as farm land and some of the land was used for agriculture. Besides mineral land, the lead region also contained rich, tillable soil situated near pleasant groves of trees. The mining towns furnished markets for the produce grown in the surrounding area. Farmers soon moved in along with the miners, and as the mines became exhausted or less profitable to work, some of the miners also turned to farming.

Since the early settlement of Wisconsin was in the south, the movement of people in the lead region, at least, was northeast rather than westerly. With the exploitation of the lead resources Americans found new opportunities in Wisconsin and for a time the lead region was the center of its economic and political activity. The lead-producing counties provided numerous territorial political leaders and their representatives influenced political affairs out of proportion to their size. The region supplied Wisconsin's territorial delegate to Congress for six years, the territorial governor for eight years, and its chief justice for twelve years, as well as a number of lesser officials.

Wisconsin's second large group of settlements centered around the Milwaukee area. Here, after 1825, settlers arrived in large numbers from the East via the Erie Canal and the Great Lakes. The two population centers were widely separated and their non-contiguous nature added another factor to Wisconsin's frontier history. Politicians, lead merchants, farmers, and businessmen all recognized the urgent need for roads and canals to connect the two sections. Although they reacted differently to specific projects according to their own needs and interests, they constantly demanded internal improvements.

Early settlements in both Wisconsin areas grew up along waterways, Milwaukee on Lake Michigan and the lead region towns along the Mississippi and its tributaries. Americans of the first half of the nineteenth century believed water routes the only feasible ones for travel and transporting goods, and frontier lines usually fanned out from the rivers and lakes. Towns and cities dotted western riverbanks and pioneer settlements penetrated their valleys. In Ohio, Cincinnati, Marietta, and Cleveland became important frontier river towns. Indiana pioneers founded Fort Wayne at the site of a military post on the portage between the Wabash and Maumee rivers, and in Michigan settlement flowed northward from the lake port of Detroit. Wisconsin's two oldest settlements, Green Bay and Prairie du Chien, were both on waterways. Later, Sheboygan, Manitowoc, and Racine grew up along Lake Michigan's shores. In the western part of the state, La Crosse became an important town on the Mississippi. While the lead region towns of Platteville, Dodgeville, and Mineral Point were not themselves on navigable streams, they depended upon the Mississippi for transportation of mineral ore to distant markets.

With increased settlement little remained of the original French influence in Wisconsin. A few fur traders and French settlers remained during the pioneer period, but many new people entered the region. Among them were the American soldiers stationed on the frontier. The Wisconsin army garrisons became the advance posts of civilization. Military men acted as law enforcement officers, construction engineers, road builders, and scientific observers of the land, its climate, and its resources. The army enforced the decisions of the Indian agents and provided a meeting place for the agents and the Indians. The agents vainly tried to regulate the Indian trade and to keep liquor away from the Indians. They also attempted to prevent squatters from moving in on land owned by the Indians or on government land before it had been surveyed and opened to settlement.

The army virtually governed early Wisconsin from three posts located within the territory. In 1816 the government constructed Fort Howard at Green Bay and Fort Crawford at Prairie du Chien, and in 1828 it added Fort Winnebago at Portage. The army was the first symbol of national law and order in the region, but it was much more than that. The officers were often men of education and means. They lived in comfort and provided an example of luxurious living on the early frontier. On occasion they held lavish balls and grand banquets. They also supported the garrison schools which were often the only schools in the area, attended by the children of those who were not connected with the fort as well as those who were.

The military posts served a number of functions on Wisconsin's frontier. Carpenters, blacksmiths, tanners, and other skilled artisans found employment at the forts. The neatly kept vegetable gardens of the posts were models of gardening. Physicians and surgeons stationed with the garrisons nearly always practiced among the neighboring civilians. The brightly uniformed regimental bands added color and gaiety as well as music to community celebrations. Settlers sometimes worshipped at the garrison chapels, and the guard houses served as county jails, housing civilian as well as military prisoners.

The military personnel, like Wisconsin's pioneer settlers, was scattered in several unconnected areas. The need for rapid communications between the forts stimulated projects for improving transportation facilities throughout the territory. The military men built bridges, drained swamplands, and cut crude trails through the wilderness. War Department contracts paid for a whole network of military roads throughout Wisconsin, Minnesota, and Iowa. James Duane Doty and others who combined politics and land speculation supported such projects by holding numerous public meetings, petitioning Washington and writing letters to the newspapers. Doty worked assiduously for the construction of a road from Fort Howard at Green Bay to Fort Winnebago at Portage. By 1837 the army had built a rough path which ran from Green Bay to Portage and from there to Prairie du Chien. Later a web of crude roads networked the settled parts of the territory, built and financed by towns, counties, and even some private individuals. Early Wisconsin roads were often little more than cleared paths, but they filled a vital need and became much traveled by thousands of immigrants as well as wagons full of lead and produce.

Military rule was sufficient for Wisconsin when few besides the Indians inhabited it. But the army was not fitted to cope with a more densely settled region. As more settlers came and the Indians moved westward, the army moved closer to the frontier. By the time of the Mexican War the garrisons had been abandoned, but not all of the men who had served in the army left the region. Some soldiers had spotted likely places to make a home and many remained to help develop the state. These people also advertised Wisconsin. Their letters, reports, and conversations promoted Wisconsin and called attention to its potentialities to Americans in other parts of the country.

Washington officials tried to negotiate treaties and move the Indians before settlers arrived, but some settlers moved into desirable tracts still in Indian country, and in the lead region early miners also encroached on Indian land. Two brief military campaigns resulted from the clash of interests. In 1827 several isolated murders of settlers by Indians and the subsequent war preparations by a group of Winnebago under Chief Red Bird from the Prairie du Chien area led to a near outbreak of warfare. But Red Bird and his braves surrendered without a fight when they found themselves caught between a pincer of American army and militia forces. Two years afterwards, at a great council held at Prairie du Chien, four Indian tribes agreed to sell the entire lead region to the United States government.

Other Indian cessions followed but squatters paid no attention to what was Indian land and what was not. New trouble broke out when Chief Black Hawk led a thousand Indians, mostly women and children, across the Mississippi River near the mouth of the Rock River in the spring of 1832. His people had moved west earlier under pressure from oncoming settlers and his aim was to return to his homeland and grow corn. The Americans viewed the peaceful Indians' movements with alarm, ordering them to turn back at Fort Armstrong (Rock Island). When Black Hawk tried to negotiate with a group of militia volunteers, the jittery settlers fired upon his truce party.

Black Hawk, Chief of the Sauk
SHSW Colls.

Forty Indians in the group returned fire and caused a
panic among the whites who reported wild stories of a
widespread Indian uprising. For several months following, Black Hawk's men raided settlements in northern Illinois and southwestern Wisconsin, killing about two hundred settlers.

In his autobiography which he dictated to Antoine Le Clair, a government Indian interpreter, Black Hawk set forth his complaints about mistreatment by the white settlers and their officials:

One of my old friends thought he was safe. His corn-field was on a small island of Rock river. He planted his corn; it came up well—but the white man saw it!—he wanted the island, and took his team over, ploughed up the corn, and re-planted it for himself! The old man shed tears; not for himself, but the distress his family would be in if they raised no corn.

The white people brought whiskey into our village, made our people drunk, and cheated them out of their horses, guns, and traps! This fraudulent system was carried to such an extent that I apprehended serious difficulties might take place, unless a stop was put to it. Consequently, I visited all the whites and begged them not to sell whiskey to my people. One of them continued the practice openly. I took a party of my young men, went to his house, and took out his barrel and broke in the head and turned out the whiskey. I did this for fear some of the whites might be killed by my people when drunk.

Our people were treated badly by the whites on many occasions. At one time, a white man beat one of our women cruelly, for pulling a few suckers of corn out of his field, to suck when hungry! At another time, one of our young men was beat with clubs by two white men for opening a fence which crossed our road, to take his horse through. His shoulder blade was broken, and his body badly bruised, from which he soon after *died!*

Bad, and cruel, as our people were treated by the whites, not one of them was hurt or molested by any of my band. I hope this will prove that we are a peaceable people—having permitted ten men to take possession of

> our corn-fields; prevent us from planting corn; burn and
> destroy our lodges; ill-treat our women; and *beat to
> death* our men, without offering resistance to their bar-
> barous cruelties. This is a lesson worthy for the white
> man to learn: to use forbearance when injured.—DONALD
> JACKSON, ED., *Black Hawk: An Autobiography* (Urbana,
> Ill., 1955), 114–115.

After eighteen militiamen under Henry Dodge fought a
skirmish on the Pecatonica River in which thirteen Indians
were killed, Black Hawk retreated up the Rock River into
the Four Lakes Region of Wisconsin. The Indians eluded
militia under Dodge and General James D. Henry and
held off the settlers at Wisconsin Heights along the Wisconsin River. Again the Indians attempted to surrender
but the whites, ignorant of Indian language, mistook the
truce talk for a war cry. Most of Black Hawk's band de-
scended the Wisconsin River on canoes and rafts borrowed from friendly Winnebago, only to be massacred by
the army garrison at Prairie du Chien. Black Hawk himself, with a small contingent of men, went overland toward the Mississippi. When he reached the river he once
more put up a white flag but a United States naval gun-
boat opened fire from the water and an advancing group
of army regulars attacked from the rear. Within three
hours more than three hundred Indians were slaughtered
by the United States forces and their Sioux Indian allies.
The Americans captured Black Hawk and took him East
before releasing him to return to his people. Indian treaties of 1832 and 1833 with the Winnebago, Chippewa, Ottawa, and Potawatomi ceded all of southern Wisconsin to
the United States. By the end of the territorial period the
Indians of Wisconsin no longer claimed title to the land.
Military expeditions against the Indians also called at-

tention to parts of Wisconsin previously unfamiliar to prospective settlers. The Black Hawk War, for instance, brought many militia volunteers into the Four Lakes region for the first time. The men who chased the Indian party across Wisconsin took careful note of the beauty and resources of the land through which they went. A few, at least, made observations which coincided with those of the official reports of early scientists who characterized the entire upper Mississippi valley as a wild place, full of savages and unfit for white settlement. One Black Hawk volunteer noted that the Four Lakes were the "most beautiful bodies of water" he had ever seen. If located anywhere else, he said, "they would be considered among the wonders of the world." "But," he continued, "the country they are situated in is not fit for any civilized nation of people to inhabit. It appears that the Almighty intended it for the children of the forest." There were some, however, who recognized the strategic position the Four Lakes region enjoyed, situated as it was between the southwestern and southeastern settlements. Four years later territorial legislators named it the future site of Wisconsin's capital.

Even during territorial days men saw different prospects in Wisconsin's future. Although the majority of those who flocked to the territory arrived from older frontier areas, most of them were native Americans. While southerners predominated in the earlier lead region settlements, many of the later Wisconsin emigrants came from the western sections of Ohio, New York, and New England. They came for various reasons but basically Wisconsin meant an opportunity for them to better their material condition. Lawyers, land speculators, businessmen, merchants, farmers, and politicians all hoped they would do better in Wisconsin than they had at home. Most of them probably did about the same. Although the frontier sometimes offered less professional competition than the more settled areas, a fourth-rate lawyer was still a fourth-rate lawyer. Most of those who attempted to "get rich quick" failed to get rich at all. Wisconsin's frontier was a haven for debtors, and in time some of them acquired new debts and then abandoned them to seek fortunes on still newer frontiers. On the other hand, careful, conservative businessmen in territorial Wisconsin, as elsewhere, could gradually accumulate wealth as well as a reputation for economic integrity.

Living conditions on the Wisconsin frontier varied considerably. There were the usual discomforts and annoyances, but the settlers never had to face the terrors of starvation. The land provided ample food for all. Early arrivals usually brought a bare minimum of furniture and some of the homes were mere wooden shanties with mud plastered between the boards to keep out wind and rain. In an amazingly short time the various towns took on the more advanced aspects of civilized communities. Schools, churches, and various public buildings appeared along with the settlers' homes. Some of the homes were just as comfortable as any in older parts of the country.

The more successful pioneers acquired large land holdings and constructed homes which, by their size and appearance, bespoke the wealth of their owners. Both the Henry S. Baird house and the James Duane Doty house at Green Bay were showplaces in their day. And even in the more remote frontier areas comfort was not unknown. Henry Gratiot built a fine stone house on his well-groomed frontier estate, Gratiot's Grove. George Wallace Jones' farm home at Sinsinawa Mound was also unusually luxurious. In 1837 George W. Featherstonhaugh visited the Jones' home and observed: "Everything in the home was the very reverse of what we had lately been accustomed to, and we sat down to a very nice repast, enliv-

In her fascinating autobiography entitled WAU-BUN, THE "EARLY DAY" IN THE NORTHWEST, *Mrs. John H. Kinzie, wife of the Indian agent at Fort Winnebago, described their living quarters at the army post:*

Our quarters were spacious, but having been constructed of the green trees of the forest, cut down and sawed into boards by the hands of the soldiers, they were considerably given to shrinking and warping, thus leaving many a yawning crevice. Stuffing the cracks with cotton batting, and pasting strips of paper over them, formed the employment of many a leisure hour.

Then the chimneys, spite of all the currents of air, which might have been expected to create a draught, had a sad habit of smoking. To remedy this, a couple of gunbarrels were, by order of the commanding officer, sawed off and inserted in the hearth, one on each side of the fireplace, in the hope that the air from the room below might help to carry the smoke into its proper place, the chimney.—LOUISE PHELPS KELLOGG, ED., Mrs. John H. Kinzie, *Wau-Bun, the "Early Day" in the Northwest* (Menasha, Wis., 1948), 83–84.

ened by the agreeable manners of the mistress of the house, and a most pleasant sister of our host who had been educated in Wales and only had just returned from a visit to England."

Often the early Wisconsin settler combined business with politics. James Duane Doty was a good example. Doty served Wisconsin Territory as governor and delegate to Congress; after statehood he served two terms in Congress. Doty was also a shrewd land speculator and always kept his landed interests in mind. A dynamic and determined person, he made a number of trips throughout Wisconsin picking out choice townsites and land for speculation. As a personal lobbyist in the first territorial legislature he played one faction against the other, distributed such favors as choice land titles, and succeeded in locating the capital at his "paper town" of Madison City in the Four Lakes region. Doty failed to gain the high political honors he coveted and eventually he sought political and economic fortune in another frontier region. In 1861 President Lincoln appointed him Indian Superintendent in Utah and two years later, governor of Utah Territory.

The shifting and unsettled nature of frontier life provided opportunities for individuals in many fields, but with the coming of more people and more stability, the chances for quick enrichment or powerful political influence lessened. Some who had come to frontier Wisconsin yielded to the hope that other frontiers would prove their making. When Charles H. Larrabee reached Wisconsin in 1847, he had already tried his luck as a law student in Ohio, a farmer-newspaperman in Mississippi, and a city attorney in Chicago. Settling in Horicon, he built some mills and speculated in land and politics. Larrabee filled a number of territorial offices including that of circuit judge, and a decade after statehood he went to Congress for a term. Larrabee was an ardent Democrat and friend of Stephen A. Douglas. He served in the Civil War, but probably because of his political connections, he never got the rank of general for which he had hoped. After the war Larrabee migrated first to California, then to Oregon, and back to California again, always hoping that the next frontier would be different from the last. To Larrabee and others like him Wisconsin offered an opportunity to succeed in politics, but that opportunity did not materialize.

There were some who arrived in Wisconsin with what seemed to be greater assets than Larrabee's. Alexander

Hamilton's son, William S. Hamilton, combined a West Point education and a famous name in American history, but Hamilton, too, found it difficult to win a political position in Wisconsin. He settled in the lead region where he developed the town of Hamilton's Diggings (later Wiota) around his smelting furnace. As a Whig he had political ambitions, but he failed to win political office and left Wisconsin for the California mining frontier during the gold rush. There he died before he had the chance to learn whether or not the people in the Far West would accord him more recognition than had the pioneers of Wisconsin.

Not all of the failures on Wisconsin's frontier left the territory. Some turned to project after project in the region itself, always trusting that the next would prove to be their making. Such a man was Moses M. Strong of Mineral Point, who came to Wisconsin from Vermont in 1836. He came to speculate in lands, but his grandiose schemes never succeeded. Other business ventures also intended for quick riches only brought Strong new debts. He became a minor figure in Wisconsin territorial politics but he never got the offices for which he longed. Strong had great dreams of wealth and power but he was not able to carry through the hard work required to give them substance. Personal weaknesses, including a mania for gambling and excessive fondness for liquor, combined to keep him from making a success of life on the Wisconsin frontier.

Some men of limited talents did succeed in acquiring political position on Wisconsin's turbulent frontier. Henry Dodge, who emigrated to the lead region in 1827, was one of them. He gained a reputation as an Indian fighter, participating as an officer in the Winnebago uprising of 1827 and the Black Hawk War five years later. Dodge mined and smelted lead in the vicinity of the present town of Dodgeville. In 1832 President Andrew Jackson appointed

Henry Dodge
SHSW Colls.

him major of a battalion of United States Mounted
Rangers that patrolled the Indian frontier of the western
plains, and the following year he named Dodge colonel of
the regiment of dragoons that replaced them. In 1836 the
President again rewarded Dodge, a loyal Democrat, by
appointing him the first governor of Wisconsin Territory.
Dodge and James Duane Doty soon found themselves at

James Duane Doty
SHSW Colls.

odds and Wisconsin territorial political factions developed around the long-lasting feud. While Dodge was governor Doty represented the territory in Congress. In 1841 the Whig President John Tyler appointed Doty governor and Wisconsin voters then elected Dodge as their delegate to Congress.

Although intense and bitter, the rivalry between Dodge

and Doty never came to blows. The avoidance of violence
was not due to any restraint on the part of Henry Dodge,
an impetuous person who was once convicted of assault

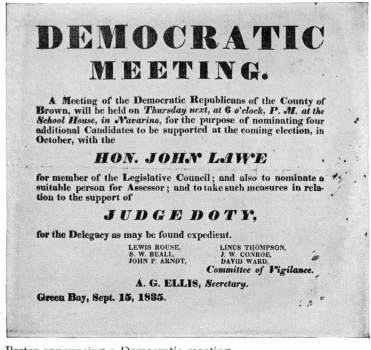

DEMOCRATIC
MEETING.

A Meeting of the Democratic Republicans of the County of
Brown, will be held on *Thursday next, at* **6** *o'clock, P. M. at the
School House, in Navarino,* for the purpose of nominating four
additional Candidates to be supported at the coming election, in
October, with the

HON. JOHN LAWE

for member of the Legislative Council; and also to nominate a
suitable person for Assessor; and to take such measures in relation to the support of

JUDGE DOTY,

for the Delegacy as may be found expedient.

LEWIS ROUSE,   LINUS THOMPSON,
S. W. BEALL,   J. W. CONROE,
JOHN P. ARNDT,   DAVID WARD,
                      Committee of Vigilance.

A. G. ELLIS, *Secretary.*

Green Bay, Sept. 15, 1835.

Poster announcing a Democratic meeting
SHSW Colls.

and battery. Another time, when a grand jury indicted
him for treason because of his connection with the Aaron
Burr conspiracy, Dodge personally quashed the indict-
ment by beating nine of the jurors. When their quarrel
began, Doty, in a series of newspaper letters, accused
Dodge of taking more credit than he deserved for the removal of the Winnebago Indians from the lead region.
Dodge nearly set out for Green Bay to right the record
and erase the insult, but some friends prevented his de-
parture.

Violence, however, was not unknown in Wisconsin's territorial politics. In 1842 a heated quarrel between two council members led to a murder in the council halls at Madison, when James R. Vineyard impulsively shot Charles C. P. Arndt. Moses M. Strong defended Vineyard before a Green County court, and the twelve jurors refused to find him guilty of manslaughter. A characteristic frontier incident, the shooting gave unwanted publicity to Wisconsin Territory. Readers throughout the country gleaned the vivid details from their local newspapers. Charles Dickens included a description of the affair in his travel book, *American Notes*, and saw in it further evidence of the degradation of men in a slave society. Vineyard was a Kentuckian and to Dickens that meant that his character had been "formed in slave districts, and brutalized by slave customs."

At the same time that men like Vineyard were given an important voice in Wisconsin's territorial affairs, others of a less tempestuous nature were working quietly to transform the frontier territory into a more stable society. Lawyers, doctors, and teachers were also cultural capitalists, bringing college educations as well as professional training to the new region. Lead smelters processed ore and shipped the product to Galena or Milwaukee. Merchants like Platteville's John H. Rountree imported manufactured goods from the eastern states and sold them to eager Wisconsin buyers. Land investors purchased land tracts from the government and resold them to farmer settlers. Many businessmen devoted their total energy to building a business, not becoming involved in politics.

There was business opportunity on the Wisconsin frontier, but the work was difficult and the hours long. One of the most significant business operations was that of the land speculator, who imported credit and capital from the East at a time when it was much needed. In 1844 Cyrus

Woodman and Cadwallader C. Washburn established a very active land agency at Mineral Point. The partners first formed a law firm but they soon abandoned "petti-

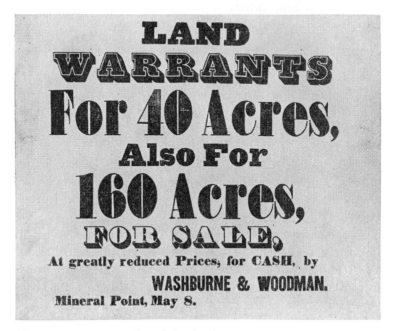

Wisconsin was covered with land sale posters.
SHSW Colls.

fogging" for selling land. They also managed land for absentee owners—checking and clearing titles, paying taxes, keeping out trespassers and selling for a profit when possible. They purchased land for others, keeping the titles in their own names until the tracts were paid for. Later they owned and operated the Helena shot tower, and ventured into banking with their Wisconsin Bank of Mineral Point. Most frontier businesses included more than one activity and the speculators were no exception. Washburn and Woodman bought and sold military land warrants, operated a mine at Dodgeville, and purchased timber lands for speculation. During the eleven years of their partnership Washburn and Woodman conducted their various business interests on conservative lines, preferring a long term, reasonable return for their investments and labor to the risks of wild schemes. They took pride in a reputation for business honesty incompatible with the fly-by-night nature of some frontier business concerns.

Woodman, especially, was proud of his business standing and he did much to help bring Wisconsin out of the frontier stage. He generously contributed land and money for churches, schools, and libraries as well as roads and bridges. He urged territorial newspaper editors to save files of their papers and contribute them to a historical library. He encouraged his western neighbors to pay their debts, develop their farms, and live more like "civilized" New Englanders. Some of his activities, like his support of internal improvements, added to the value of his land holdings and his business. Businessmen like Woodman performed a service to the frontier region which was less glamorous and exciting than the military and political services of men like Henry Dodge, but at the same time was just as lasting in its impact.

Some land speculators were also town promoters who played an important role in early Wisconsin history. Frontier towns did not appear by magic at strategic points. Behind most such settlements was an individual or a group of people who saw the possibilities of a town, advertised the place, and helped to build it. By word and deed they advertised the young settlements, providing capital for their early nurture and attracting merchants, skilled workers, and professional men to serve what they hoped would become a rapidly growing population. Many of the territory's early leaders had special interest in one or another of the region's new towns. Solomon Juneau, a fur trader and merchant, in financial partnership with Morgan L. Martin owned much of Milwaukee which the two hoped would become Lake Michigan's major port. Byron Kilbourn developed the west side of Milwaukee, and George H. Walker owned another tract to the south. But the territory's first capital, Belmont, never attained the importance that its boosters hoped for, and there were other towns that never left the paper stage.

The nature of Wisconsin settlement helped determine the site of the capital. The decision was a most important one for the first territorial legislature meeting at Belmont in 1836. Each lead region village had its group of hopeful boosters as did nearly every other town and paper town in the territory. Although the wily methods, charming manners, and generous gifts of James Duane Doty (who owned the site which became Madison) played a large part in the decision, the location of the capital was a compromise. Madison lay between the two population groups. It was a logical choice, and not all those who finally voted for it had received town lots from Doty. The large Iowa delegation favored Madison, realizing that it would further their own ambitions to establish a separate territory west of the Mississippi. The decision made, Madison quickly emerged from the paper stage into a thriving town.

The location of roads, canals, and harbor improvements all gave certain towns an advantage in the economic rivalry in frontier Wisconsin. So did the location of government land offices. In 1834 the federal government opened land offices in Mineral Point and Green Bay, and four years later in Milwaukee. With increased settlement the offices moved to other, less settled parts of the territory. Before the land could be sold, the Indian titles in the area had to be cleared; later, surveyors platted the region and the land tracts were sold at public auction. The land office attracted settlers, lawyers, merchants, money lend-ers, and speculators. They brought business to the town during its early formative period, but the advantage only lasted until the people of the town where the office was located could develop new resources. Long after the original three land offices closed their books, Milwaukee and Green Bay continued to be significant Wisconsin communities, but Mineral Point never enjoyed equal growth and importance.

The increase in the number of Wisconsin towns added to already existing demands for internal improvements. Behind each plan for a canal, road, or harbor was a town and its promoters. During the territorial era internal improvements in Wisconsin had meaning mostly in relation to hopes for the future. There was much talk and little accomplishment. Byron Kilbourn's ambitious plan for a Rock River canal connecting Milwaukee with the Mississippi got so far as to receive help in the form of a government land grant, which the territorial legislature accepted and began to sell. But the project floundered on the rocks of the Panic of 1837 and Governor Doty's consistent opposition. Only one small section of the canal was actually dug.

Morgan L. Martin was just as determined as Kilbourn, with his project for improving the Fox-Wisconsin River route to the Mississippi. Residents of Green Bay and other key points along the two rivers added enthusiastic support to the Fox-Wisconsin project. In 1846 Congress lent support with a land grant, but it was not until after Wisconsin became a state that any work was done on it.

Some settlers in Wisconsin Territory thought plank roads and railroads more valuable than river and canal improvements. But only a few plank roads were built before statehood, and the railroad arrived even later. The rivers and lakes continued to be important. Mississippi River steamboats connected Wisconsin with the Gulf of

Mexico, and as early as 1834 steamboats brought immigrants and goods into the territory from the East via the Great Lakes. Territorial requests for federal aid had only meager results. Besides building a lighthouse at Milwaukee in 1838, the federal government did little except supplement the small amounts spent by the port towns to build and improve their harbor facilities. The problems of the people in Wisconsin Territory were primarily local problems and they had to cope with them with a minimum of aid from the federal government.

AN IMMIGRANT'S VIEW OF WISCONSIN

Those who emigrated from the Old World to Wisconsin often recorded their observations and thoughts in letters to friends and relatives back home. The following description is from a letter written in 1847 in Baraboo by John Owen, a Welsh immigrant, to his brother in Wales:
The land in general is exceptionally good, and although thousands come here the country is so immense that there is yet plenty of government land. There are miles of it near me not yet taken. Many have come here since I came, but we were the first Welsh family to cross the Wisconsin River. It is difficult to obtain government land without paying a higher price for it than the government price. The natives are grasping, claiming the land before the Welsh. The Welsh settle before they go far enough into the interior to find government land, the price of which is 5s. 3d. of your money.—WILBUR S. SHEPPERSON, "The Natives Are Grasping; A Welshman's Letter from Wisconsin," in the *Wisconsin Magazine of History*, 43:130–131 (Winter, 1959–1960).

Not all those who came to frontier Wisconsin were from other parts of the United States. Foreign immigrants also saw opportunity for a better life in the frontier region. More than half the immigrants were British. News of the mineral region and its rich resources reached England at just about the time that many of the Cornish tin mines no longer produced profitable yields, and around 1835 Cornish miners began to enter the lead region. The Cornish were highly skilled miners, and they introduced techniques of deep mining that vastly increased the amount of lead taken from the Wisconsin mines. Their peculiar dialect and small, neat stone houses soon characterized a segment of life in the territory's mining frontier. Besides the Cornish miners and other British immigrants, others, including Germans, Norwegians, and Swiss, came to Wisconsin Territory. The Norwegians tended to settle in farming country in the south and the Germans clustered around Milwaukee and along Lake Michigan. Although they faced the task of mastering a new language and learning new customs, these Europeans quickly adapted themselves to the land and society of the frontier territory of their choice. Basically, Wisconsin offered the same opportunity for the immigrants that it had for Americans from other parts of the land. "If I was asked the question whether this country or my native land I liked the best or which I should prefer," wrote an English immigrant to his father back home, "I should answer Decidedly this though I love my native land as the place of my birth." His sentiments were probably those of many others.

Most of the immigrants accepted the ideals and ideas of the majority of Americans. Some immigrants and some Americans, however, found in the various American frontiers opportunity for social experimentation, for the attempted creation of a perfect society in a worldly setting. In frontier Indiana Father George Rapp, a leader of devout German religious communitarians, found what appeared to be an ideal location for his society and the group moved there in 1815 from an earlier home in western Pennsylvania. After only a decade Rapp sold the property to the Welsh reformer and industrialist Robert Owen, who changed the name from Harmony to New Harmony and quickly established a community that had neither harmony nor economic success. In frontier Ohio and Kentucky the Shakers practiced their peculiar variety of religious communism, renouncing family life as well as private property.

Wisconsin's Ceresco was another frontier community experiment. In 1844, seventy-one members established a joint stock company to finance a community on the present site of Ripon. Among them was the erratic follower of many causes, Warren Chase. Their professed objects were "the prosecution of agriculture, manufactures, commerce, the arts and sciences, education and domestic industry, according to the system of Charles Fourier as near as may be possible." Fourier, a French social philosopher, had written a blueprint for a new organization of society composed of closely-knit communities or phalanxes with a maximum amount of group living. The Wisconsin communitarians agreed to refrain from "rude and indecent behavior, profane swearing," lying, stealing, and gambling. They hoped to create a world within the frontier world, and their attempt to do so added to the meaning of territorial Wisconsin. Here was a place where even the social innovator could attempt to live his peculiar way of life in peace.

Ceresco both succeeded and failed. Its economic picture was bright. The communitarians put up unusually large and well constructed buildings and mills; they grew fine crops on more than a thousand acres of well tilled fields. Yet within a year most of them had abandoned the community dining hall for their family dinner tables, and in 1849 they got permission from the legislature to sell the property and divide the proceeds. Not all the members had joined for idealistic reasons and when they came to believe that more opportunity lay outside the phalanx than within, they favored a return to individualism. Some former members bought newly opened land along the Fox River and continued the same successful farming operations that they had practiced while in Ceresco. The lure of more conventional economic opportunity on the Wisconsin frontier proved stronger than the bonds of the communitarian ideal.

Ceresco was a social experiment. The Wisconsin frontier also attracted some religious non-conformists like the fanatical James Jesse Strang who, although a very recent convert to Mormonism at the time of Joseph Smith's murder in 1844, claimed to be his duly appointed successor. Strang convinced some members of the Mormon faith that his credentials were valid, and persuaded them to follow him instead of Brigham Young and the large group he led to Utah. The Strang Mormons established a religious community called Voree, the Garden of Peace, near Burlington, Wisconsin. Six years later the Mormon leader moved his flock to Beaver Island in the northern part of Lake Michigan where he instituted polygamy and became a "king" as well as a prophet. The Mormon monarchy soon aroused the ire and opposition of its neighbors and after a half dozen years they destroyed its property and murdered its leader. Strang's pattern of living deviated too much from conventional lines, even in frontier Wisconsin and Michigan. The opportunity for religious pioneers in frontier Wisconsin was clearly limited by the traditions of its other inhabitants.

Meanwhile settlers continued to enter the territory both in the lead region and in the eastern section. By 1846 155,000 people lived in Wisconsin and by 1850 nearly twice that many. With the population growth had come changes in governmental structure. From 1800 to 1809 Wisconsin had been part of Indiana Territory, from 1809 to 1818 it was included in Illinois Territory, and it was in Michigan Territory from 1818 to 1836, when Wisconsin Territory was created. For its first two years Wisconsin Territory included considerable land west of the Mississippi in the later states of Iowa, Minnesota, and the Dakotas. Wisconsin residents skipped the first, most autocratic, stage of territorial government as provided in the Northwest Ordinance of 1787, and began their territorial experience with the second stage. It provided an appointed governor and council along with an elected lower house of the legislature, and a nonvoting delegate to Congress. Most Wisconsin territorial politicians called themselves Jacksonians until 1841, when the Whigs organized an opposi-

---

THE END OF STRANG'S MORMON KINGDOM

In June, 1856, two renegade Mormons fatally shot James Jesse Strang and then fled from Beaver Island on the steamer MICHIGAN *as previously planned. Within a few months groups of anti-Mormons ousted all of Strang's followers from the island settlement. A correspondent of the Green Bay* ADVOCATE *accompanied the mob and reported the final operations from the* MICHIGAN:

You would pronounce us a very brave and warlike people, returning from the seat of war with . . . our stacks of arms and our loud boasting of feats performed, and threats to be executed.

I assure you, in all soberness, matters are . . . desperate hereaway, and it would be no seven days' wonder if all our Mormon friends at the Beavers were . . . completely routed and "cleaned out" from the Island. The Sheriff from Mackinac with his posse of about 30 men, mostly collected at the [Green] Bay and Washington Island [on the lake-side of Green Bay], have taken five of

---

the Mormon gang and two more for witnesses. Some shots were fired and some kicks and cuffs exchanged. . . . Good and strong resistance was offered—but to no purpose—they had to come aboard dead or alive, and from the actions of some of the posse, I judged they cared mighty little which. . . .

The plan now is to return this week if possible and clear every Mormon from the island—peaceably [or] . . . at the range of the rifle. God help the Mormons . . . if half of their wrongs and grievances be true. The Mormon Kingdom then richly deserves such a fate. . . .

Quite Kansas like? Eh! Rich—Rich! you may believe, has been this day's sights. I shall not be "after" forgetting it very soon.

Yours Patriotically,

GREEN BAY.

CHARLES O. BURGESS, "Green Bay and the Mormons of Beaver Island," in the *Wisconsin Magazine of History,* 42:46 (Autumn, 1958).

tion group along national party lines. The political leaders, however, emphasized local rather than national issues.

With each passing year settlers arrived in Wisconsin in larger numbers, entering land, establishing businesses, providing the bricks and mortar with which to build a state. Southern Wisconsin ceased to be a frontier and the line of settlement moved northward. In time the settlers filled in the gap between the lead region and the southeastern settlements. In the older sections the people became more settled and the towns more stable. The rougher aspects of frontier life disappeared. An ever growing number of towns boasted of something resembling schools and libraries. Episcopal, Methodist, Baptist, Congregational, Lutheran, and Presbyterian ministers competed with the Catholic priests for the souls of the inhabitants. Each group had its own churches, adding another stabilizing institution to Wisconsin towns. The outward signs of civilization appeared. Wisconsin continued to offer seemingly unlimited opportunity to its many immigrants as well as for the eastern creditors who financed so much of its early activity. And with its constant growth in size and its striving for political maturity Wisconsin's territorial government could no longer fill the need. There was in the territory a combination of natural and human resources that provided ample material for a significant future after statehood.

SUGGESTED ADDITIONAL READING

Campbell, Henry C. *Wisconsin in Three Centuries, 1634–1905* (4 vols., New York, 1906), II, 159–311.
Clark, James I. *The Wisconsin Lead Region: Frontier Community* (Madison, 1955).
——————. *Henry Dodge: Frontiersman* (Madison, 1957).
Conan, Bryant Eaton. "A King Sleeps in Wisconsin," in the *Wisconsin Magazine of History*, 40:107–112 (Winter, 1956–1957).
Curti, Merle E., et. al. *The Making of an American Community: A Case Study of Democracy in a Frontier County* (Stanford, 1959).
Duckett, Kenneth W. *Frontiersman of Fortune: Moses M. Strong of Mineral Point* (Madison, 1955).
Gara, Larry. *Westernized Yankee: The Story of Cyrus Woodman* (Madison, 1956).
Mrs. John H. Kinzie. *Wau-Bun, The "Early Day" in the Northwest* (Menasha, Wis., 1948).
McIntosh, Montgomery E. "Cooperative Communities in Wisconsin," in the *Proceedings of the State Historical Society of Wisconsin*, 1903:99–117.
Pedrick, S. M. "The Wisconsin Phalanx at Ceresco," in the *Proceedings of the State Historical Society of Wisconsin*, 1903:190–226.
Prucha, Francis Paul. *Broadax and Bayonet: The Role of the*

United States Army in the Development of the Northwest, 1815–1860 (Madison, 1953).

Quaife, Milo M. *Wisconsin, Its History and Its People, 1634–1924* (4 vols., Chicago, 1924), I, 361–472.

———. *The Kingdom of Saint James: A Narrative of the Mormons* (New Haven, 1930).

Raney, William Francis. *Wisconsin: A Story of Progress* (New York, 1940), 64–121.

Rooney, Elizabeth B. "The Story of the Black Hawk War," in the *Wisconsin Magazine of History,* 40:274–283 (Summer, 1957).

Schafer, Joseph. *The Wisconsin Lead Region* (Madison, 1932).

Smith, Alice E. *James Duane Doty: Frontier Promoter* (Madison, 1954).

———. "James Duane Doty: Mephistopheles in Wisconsin," in the *Wisconsin Magazine of History,* 34:195–198, 238–240 (Summer, 1951).

Still, Bayrd, *Milwaukee: The History of a City* (Madison, 1948), 3–108.

CHAPTER 3

Wisconsin as a New State
1848–1860

In 1848 Wisconsin became the nation's thirtieth state. In the era just before the Civil War statehood had special importance. Traditionally, the states were almost sovereign. Governors, legislators, and state judges made significant decisions and wielded considerable power. Those who favored Wisconsin statehood assumed that the problems faced by residents of the area would materially diminish when the territory became a state. There was little realistic basis for such hopes. Wisconsin's pioneer residents soon learned that many of their difficulties persisted, despite the governmental transformation from territory to state.

Statehood had economic as well as political significance. Business progress lagged in territorial days. Eastern creditors grudgingly invested only small sums in western business enterprises. The Panic of 1837, with its aftermath of western states' repudiating their debts and declaring their bonds worth little or nothing, frightened the financiers of

---

AN ARGUMENT FOR STATEHOOD

Prior to Wisconsin's becoming a state many of the territory's newspapers carried editorials and reports which set forth the advantages of such a change. The following was published as "Advice to the Legislature," in the Southport AMERICAN, *December 6, 1845:*

The people of this territory are now, as we believe, fully convinced that they are old enough, and rich enough, and strong enough to take care of themselves, and this position attained, what earthly reason can there be for our remaining longer in a state of vassalage— beggars at the national treasury for the poor pittance of appropriation for the expenses of the government, so grudgingly bestowed—and forgoing, for the sake of it, the right and all the advantages of electing our executive officers, framing our own judiciary, and being really *represented*, and by the number of votes to which we are entitled, in the national councils.

New York and New England. Lax western banking laws made conservative Eastern bankers wary of bank notes from the West. Heavy losses from foolish western speculative land investments made the money changers even more timid. The flow of credit westward became a mere trickle at the very time Wisconsinites most desperately needed help to construct harbors, canals, roads, and railroads. While these problems were common in all parts of the West, many Wisconsin settlers thought statehood would solve them. As a state Wisconsin would be able to charter transportation companies and encourage the building of internal improvements. Loosed from the ties of territorial dependence, Wisconsin citizens could provide their own laws and make their own decisions. Eastern investors, argued many, would then look more favorably on Wisconsin.

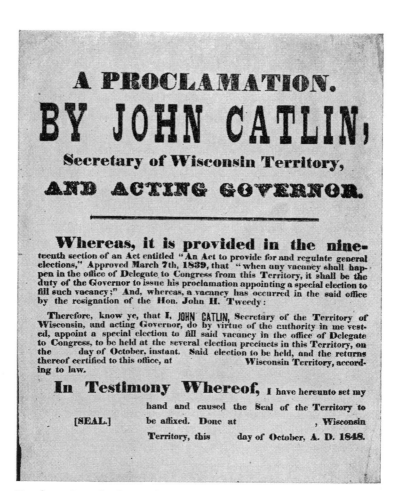

Proclamation of John Catlin, 1848
SHSW Colls.

Long before it became a popular issue the movement for Wisconsin statehood had gained the support of the territorial governors. Other politicians quickly responded. The prospect of numerous state offices and the accompanying patronage they would offer whetted the appetites of office seekers. However, many settlers in Wisconsin Territory cared little about what kind of government they had. Many of the qualified voters never bothered to cast ballots in the various elections concerning statehood and the two proposed constitutions. Some Wisconsin settlers looked upon all government as, at best, a necessary evil. In 1843 an English immigrant wrote home from Wisconsin Territory, "Politicks are a subject that we are never troubled with hear [sic] and we might be without a government for any trouble or expenc[e] they are to us." They had no policemen nor Poor Law Commissioners and were not often bothered by tax gatherers. Instead of a class of privileged rulers, the local officials in Wisconsin Territory were all working men; "if the[y] wont work they must not eat." Such limited government seemed almost utopian to European settlers who sought individual freedom as well as economic betterment in frontier Wisconsin.

The very condition of minimum government that appeared attractive to frontier farmers annoyed some political leaders and businessmen. They recognized a need for more (and more efficient) government in a region that was rapidly developing economically. Many of the politicians were also businessmen. Territorial officials were often land speculators, the owners of mining machinery and smelting furnaces, town promoters, lumbermen, or merchants. Those not directly involved in one or another of Wisconsin's rapidly multiplying enterprises also recognized the important relation between statehood and economic development. In a short message urging a referendum on statehood to the Legislative Assembly in 1846,

Pioneer's cabin in Wisconsin—sketch by Wengler
SHSW Colls.

Governor Henry Dodge called attention to the Wisconsin farmers who were "rapidly developing the agricultural resources of the territory" and converting the prairies into "luxuriant fields," the "inexhaustible stores of mineral wealth," the "salubrious climate," the soil which was "suited to the production of everything necessary for the comfort of man," and to the highway of lakes and rivers bordering and net-working the territory. "With a population intelligent, industrious, and enterprising, the growth and prosperity of Wisconsin must be onward," continued the governor, "and the time is not far distant when she will form one of the most populous states of the Union."

Prior to 1846 the voters had turned down proposals for statehood four different times. Those refusals had stemmed from the inability of Governor James Duane Doty to get along with his territorial legislature, a continued insistence by Doty and others that Wisconsin should include the debt-ridden section of northern Illinois, and a popular suspicion that statehood would inevitably increase taxes and bring more government interference into the lives of the people. But in April of 1846 enough of the Territory's voters accepted Dodge's roseate view of the future to carry an election for statehood and call a constitutional convention.

Menominee Indians—sketch by Wengler
SHSW Colls.

Some foreign immigrants, especially the Germans, favored statehood because to them it represented enfranchisement and an opportunity to participate in American political life. Many other settlers also supported the move to make Wisconsin a state. Farmers and lead miners as well as merchants and town promoters looked upon internal improvements as the answer to many of their economic problems. Whatever the form such improvements might take, residents of Wisconsin hoped that they would bring new settlers, credit, and manufactured items into the territory as well as enable wheat, lumber, lead, and other products to be shipped out. As a territory Wisconsin relied upon federal grants, but under James K. Polk's administration very little money from the national treasury found its way into the Northwest. Memorials and resolutions from the legislatures as well as requests from Wisconsin's delegates in Congress fell on deaf ears, partly, thought some, because their delegates could not vote and they themselves could take no part in national elections. With statehood would come political bargaining power in addition to 500,000 acres of land from the public domain to subsidize internal improvement projects.

It soon became apparent, however, that the way to statehood was far from smooth. In the summer of 1846 Congress passed an enabling act which made provision for establishing a state government. President Polk signed the measure on August 6, 1846, and Governor Dodge called a constitutional convention in Madison for the fall. The 124 elected delegates to the convention argued for ten weeks before they emerged with a constitution. Most of them were Democrats, but the Wisconsin Democracy consisted of many warring factions. Hunkers, barnburners, tadpoles, progressives, hards, and softs, all were words suggesting various shades of Democratic Party thought on such questions as banking, the protection of homesteads against creditors, property rights for women, and immigrant suffrage. There were also lead-region versus lake-region factions and, of course, factions connected with key territorial leaders like Henry Dodge and James D. Doty.

A few leaders in the convention promoted extremist measures. Edward G. Ryan of Racine, for example, voiced the western prejudice against banks and succeeded in inserting an ironclad anti-banking clause into the constitution, thus alienating both the Whigs and the more moderate anti-banking members of the convention. Ryan refused to grant the smallest concession on a banking issue and wholly opposed those members who would permit on a trial basis a free banking system just adopted by New York. "I belong to that party which would give to banking no quarter," roared Ryan.

Moses M. Strong of Mineral Point also used the convention floor to express his version of Democratic ideas. As a member of the hunkers, or older Democratic faction, he accused some members of the convention of attempting to create a new set of leaders. Strong spoke frequently in the convention and on one occasion he charged that some in the gathering were neglecting important business while they tried "to make big men out of little ones, and little men out of big ones."

Despite their differences, however, the delegates finally agreed on a constitution. The document forbade all banks and limited the circulation of small denominations of paper money, protected the homestead of the debtor, and permitted married women to hold property in their own names. The judiciary was to be elective. Immigrants could vote, but the question of Negro suffrage was postponed for a popular referendum. Because of disastrous experiences of neighboring states with legislative spending, the legislature was severely limited in power and could not use state money for internal improvements. The state debt was not to exceed $100,000. In general, the constitution of 1846 appealed to the younger and more ambitious faction of the Democratic Party.

Few were satisfied with the entire constitution. The extreme anti-banking clause antagonized many Democrats, and conservative businessmen of both parties were shocked at measures that might impede the collection of debts. Some favored acceptance of the constitution in the hope that the obnoxious features would soon be dropped. But the movement for a second convention gained momentum before the voters had decided to reject or accept the first one. Marshall M. Strong of Racine left the convention in a huff to help defeat the constitution and prepare the way for another one. A correspondent for the Madison *Argus* applauded Strong's act, commenting, "To him chiefly will belong the honor of saving 'our beloved Wisconsin' from being converted into a Fourier phalanx playground for lunatics and idiots." Basically, the constitution seemed too unlike those of other states to win popular approval. The voting on the document was light, but in April of 1847 about six thousand more electors voted against it than for it.

A new convention met in December, 1847, and within seven weeks had prepared a new constitution. This group of sixty-nine delegates was but half the size of the first one. Two-thirds were Democrats but very few had sat in the previous gathering. The delegates were determined to produce a document acceptable to the electorate before the presidential election of 1848. The constitution was a more moderate one and the outstanding controversial questions were settled by compromise. Supporters of homestead exemption reworded the earlier article and transferred it to the bill of rights. The constitution made no mention of property rights for women. Later legislation granted such rights. A liberal suffrage clause appealed to immigrant support for the constitution. Only the banking article was fundamentally changed. The delegates dodged the issue by submitting the matter for a popular vote, and providing for a general banking law if the voters chose to have banks. Wisconsin voters accepted the new constitution in March, 1848. Even fewer electors bothered to vote than had cast ballots the previous year, but 16,417 favored ratification compared to 6,174 who opposed it.

TERMS OF WISCONSIN'S GOVERNORS, 1848–1862

June, 1848–1852	Nelson Dewey (Democrat)
January, 1852–1854	Leonard J. Farwell (Whig)
January, 1854–1856	William A. Barstow (Democrat)
March, 1856–1858	Coles Bashford (Republican) *
January, 1858–1862	Alexander W. Randall (Republican)

—*Wisconsin Blue Book*, 1915 (Madison, 1915), 367.
* In 1856 the Wisconsin Supreme Court set aside, on grounds of election irregularities, a certificate from the State Board of Canvassers which declared that Barstow was elected, and ruled in favor of Bashford.

Those who had high hopes for great progress under the self-government of statehood were disappointed. Bitter factionalism continued to harass the Democratic political leaders and eventually led to the complete disintegration of the party in the state. Personal politics along with widespread graft and corruption by state officials disillusioned the people of Wisconsin and discredited the state elsewhere. Incident after incident further exposed the inadequacies of the political leadership in the new state. In 1853 an attempt to impeach Circuit Court Justice Levi

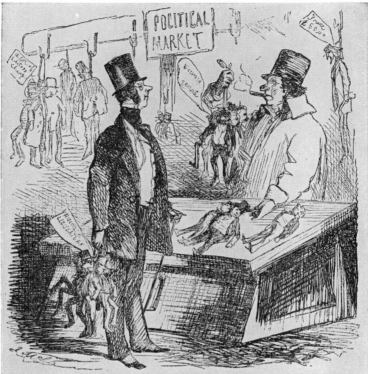

POLITICAL MARKET.

CONSCIENTIOUS RAIL-ROAD PRESIDENT to DEALER. "Ah! let me see. I think I'll take this bunch of Legislators at $5000 a head. The Senators, at—what price did you say?"

DEALER. "Can't afford 'em less than $10,000 each."

R. R. P. "Well, hand them over. I suppose I'll have to take the lot."

DEALER. "Any thing else to-day. I have a Lot of Editors, at various prices, from a Thousand down to Fifty Cents."

R. R. P. "No, nothing in that way, to-day. But I want a Governor very much indeed, and will stand $50,000 for him. Get me a Wisconsin one, if possible!"

Wisconsin politics was the subject of such satirical cartoons. *From* HARPER'S WEEKLY, *June 12, 1858.*

Hubbell on charges of bribery, embezzlement, and abuse of authority revealed the nature of Democratic factional rivalry and sowed seeds of suspicion about the court itself. The scramble to loot the state treasury popularized such catch phrases as "Barstow and the balance," and the "Forty Thieves." The former phrase derived from a private letter from a bidder for the state printing contract who vowed to get the contract if he had "to buy up Barstow and the balance" of those on the printing commission. Governor William A. Barstow's enemies charged that he plundered the school fund, catered to large-scale land speculators, profiteered from railroad charters, and stuffed his pockets with money appropriated for the construction of an insane asylum. Barstow's faction of the Democratic Party composed the "Forty Thieves," and Republican opponents claimed that their thievery culminated in a fraudulent attempt to steal the election of 1855 from the Republican victor, Coles Bashford. However, the state supreme court, called in to settle the dispute, declared in favor of Bashford and thus paved the way for new scandals under the new "reform" administration.

The era of corruption continued. Opportunity for large-scale graft came in 1856 with Wisconsin's first congressional land grant for railroad construction. Part of the grant went to Byron Kilbourn's La Crosse and Milwaukee Railroad, which had already squandered the stockholders' funds until it verged on bankruptcy. The railroad desperately needed the grant and distributed $900,000 worth of stocks and bonds to get it. Most Wisconsin legislators and state officers accepted the railroad's generous gifts. Governor Bashford got $50,000 worth of securities and shrewdly turned them in for $15,000 in cash before the road went bankrupt two years later. In 1858 a legislative investigation exposed the sordid affair and further discredited railroad companies and Wisconsin politicians.

The great hopes for economic salvation through railroad building in the new state were quickly shattered. Wisconsin legislators granted charters freely, but only a few of the companies ever built a road. Some Wisconsin towns grew up along the railroads, but others suffered for lack of direct connection. Even in places serviced by a

Prairie du Chien in 1850—sketch by Wengler
SHSW Colls.

road, farmers did not magically get rid of all their problems as overenthusiastic and unscrupulous promoters had promised. Construction only crept along. Constitutional restrictions prevented the use of state funds for internal improvements, and eastern capitalists, recalling earlier losses from western investments, hesitated to invest heavily in western railroads. Yet zealous company agents succeeded in convincing Wisconsin settlers that they must back the roads. Thousands of farmers mortgaged their homes and farms to purchase railroad stock. By the spring of 1857 the Milwaukee and Mississippi reached the river at Prairie du Chien, spanning the width of the state. Enthusiastic citizens celebrated the event with parades and bonfires, but their rejoicing was premature.

The Panic of 1857 quickly changed the mood from optimism to gloom. Bankruptcy came to all Wisconsin railroad companies, and the stocks for which the farmers had mortgaged their property were worth little or nothing. Those who were trying to sell railroad securities in the East found no market for them ."The state of the times for railroad operations," reported an agent for Wisconsin's railroads in July of 1857, "is frightful and the prospect is dubious in the extreme." No matter how low they were priced people did not want the securities. "People have been humbugged too much and disappointed so often in railroad investments," he lamented, "that they have come to regard them all as valueless. You cannot reason with them and they cannot discriminate." Such financial stringency brought a halt to Wisconsin's railroad expansion. By 1860 only nine hundred miles of railroad existed in the state.

Some credit for railroad building came from the banks that were permitted by the constitution of 1848 and later approved by Wisconsin's voters. After 1853 banking was legal in the state and bankers made loans to farmers, lumbermen, meat packers, insurance companies, and breweries in the growing state. It was a time of easy credit in Wisconsin. In addition, bank notes from other places, including "wildcats" from distantly located banks, often passed at par value. Wildcat money referred to notes from banks of dubious credit located in states with lax banking laws and situated in out-of-the-way places so that the notes could not easily be presented for redemption. Conservative bankers and those who themselves wanted to have a near monopoly on the region's finances attempted

Madison in 1850—sketch by Wengler

Milwaukee in 1850—sketch by Wengler
SHSW Colls.

to drive the wildcat currency out of the state. In 1855 a campaign organized and led by Cyrus Woodman and C. C. Washburn of Mineral Point succeeded in ridding the state of wildcat money issued by George Smith, a shrewd Scottish immigrant who operated a chain of banks. But bank notes of even more dubious value came into the state from time to time, furnishing a circulating medium for many in the Badger State but irritating the more cautious banking interests. Without some kind of centralized control to check the aggressive tactics of bankers in states with lax banking laws, the wildcats would always pose a threat to conservative bankers. The soundness of Wisconsin's own regulated banking system seemed confirmed when all the state-chartered banks successfully weathered the economic storm caused by the Panic of 1857.

If the results of statehood fell far short of the anticipations of Wisconsin's bankers, farmers, and businessmen, equal disappointment came to those who concerned themselves with cultural institutions. Many of the New Englanders among Wisconsin's settlers were ardent in their support of the idea of public education, but in practice the principle took hold very slowly. The constitution made provision for a state university and for a system of free common schools, to be supported by local taxes, interest from a school fund created by the sale of public lands, and money derived from fines and forfeitures. The constitution provided for an elected state superintendent who was to encourage education and allot the income from the school fund according to the number of pupils in each district. At first it was the local town superintendent who had the authority to license and hire teachers, and supervise the schools. By terms of a new law in 1862 the more than seven hundred town superintendents relinquished their authority to sixty county superintendents.

Yankee emigrants were shocked at the conditions in Wisconsin's schools. Only a few communities like Racine and Kenosha had schools comparable with those in parts of the East. Teachers were scarce and those who were available were often just out of school themselves. Usually they taught several grades in crowded schoolhouses. The people of Madison and Milwaukee sometimes sent their children to private schools because the public institutions had no more room. The lead region schools were so inadequate that some children attended private boarding schools in Illinois or other nearby states.

Little change came before the Civil War, even though the various state superintendents of public instruction lent support to those citizens who demanded improved schools. In his annual report for 1858 state superintendent Lyman C. Draper reported that approximately a third of Wisconsin's youngsters did not attend any school and for those who did the average school year was five and three-fifths months. Yet, noted the superintendent, this was better than before. He saw progress in the improvement of teachers' salaries, training, and professional activities. "The good work," wrote Draper, "is gradually advancing and improving."

DRAPER'S SUGGESTIONS TO IMPROVE WISCONSIN SCHOOLS

In his annual report for 1858, Lyman C. Draper, state superintendent of schools, made the following recommendations for improving education in Wisconsin:

Thus I have recommended the concentration of School Libraries into a single collection for each town, thus increasing their power for good six-fold, and lessening the number of Librarians from nearly four thousand, if each district had one, to about six hundred and fifty. Thus have I urged the adoption of the system of County Superintendents, and a County Examining Board, and the total abrogation of the district system, to be supplanted by the simpler, cheaper, and more efficient Township system—thus while creating about 1,250 new school officers in the whole State, at the same time doing away with 11,400 others, showing a clear diminution of over ten thousand officers; and providing for a more economical, more equal, and better grade of public education—better teachers, better school-houses, and better supervision; and above all, cutting up by the roots the suicidal policy of dividing and ensmalling districts, and leaving all to attend freely, 'without money and without price,' whatever school should be most convenient to them, without regard to arbitrary district, township, or county lines. Thus, also, have I urged the concentration of the management of the State University, the Normal Schools, and, to some extent, the Common Schools, also, in a Single State Board of Education, so as to adjust and har-

> monize the entire system of public education as whole
> —and not parcel out these mighty interests to different
> Boards, who might, and doubtless frequently would, en-
> tertain and put into practice diversified, and perhaps
> even clashing, methods of accomplishing the objects
> committed to their charge.—LYMAN C. DRAPER, *Tenth
> Annual Report on the Condition and Improvement of
> the Common Schools and Educational Interests of the
> State of Wisconsin, for the Year 1858* (Madison, 1858),
> 179.

The advance was gradual indeed, especially when it involved expenditure by the state. The legislature refused
to set up normal schools for training teachers. Instead, in
1856 it added a normal department, consisting of one
part-time teacher, to the university. Much of the proceeds
from the sale of Wisconsin's school lands never got near
an institution of learning. The money became a small
loan fund with most of the loans going to Democratic
Party functionaries. Many of the loans were never repaid.

Higher education received even less support from the
state. The legislature established the University of Wisconsin in 1848, but no college classes met until two years
later. During its first dozen years the struggling university
received no money from the legislature and had to construct its first buildings and pay its handful of faculty
members with borrowed funds. Some of the early regents
seemed to be more interested in promoting denomina-
tional colleges than in developing the university, and
many Wisconsinites preferred the education offered to
their children at private colleges in Appleton, Waukesha,
Ripon, or Beloit.

At least one significant Wisconsin cultural institution
began to thrive under early state sponsorship. In 1853 the
legislature chartered, and thus gave new life to, an en-

feebled State Historical Society. Two years later it added a small allotment for its library and corresponding secretary. It was Lyman C. Draper, the corresponding secre-

Lyman Copeland Draper
SHSW Colls.

tary, however, who created an important institution from these small beginnings. Even before coming to Wisconsin, Draper had outlined a series of biographical studies designed to rescue the heroes of western border warfare from oblivion. Draper never completed any of his lives of pioneers, but his collection of manuscripts formed one of the most significant bodies of papers on western history and provided countless scholars of a later day with invaluable raw materials for historical writing. Besides building a great collection, Draper built a great historical society. His energy seemed boundless, and with limited funds he succeeded in systematically collecting manuscripts, books, newspapers, and portraits. He edited and published ten volumes of valuable source materials for Wisconsin history in the Society's *Collections*. He obtained the support of many others who were also concerned with the cause of history. Draper's efforts soon won him recognition outside the state and the Society he fostered also attracted national attention to Wisconsin, but in its early years those who thought of the Society always thought of Draper. He was "a Historical Society in himself," commented the Chicago *Tribune*.

Lyman Draper brought his avid interest in history and talent for collecting manuscripts with him when he emigrated from the East. Other Yankee immigrants transplanted similar cultural capital which they invested in the new state. Some, like the nationally famed scholar Henry Barnard, who accepted a position as Chancellor of the University of Wisconsin in 1858, remained only a few years and made little impact on the state. Others who had emigrated to Wisconsin Territory stayed to help develop the region's economic resources and budding cultural institutions after Wisconsin became a state. The scientist Increase A. Lapham attracted others to Wisconsin with his promotional *Gazetteer of Wisconsin* and his continually growing fame as a publishing scholar in the fields of geology, botany, conchology, meteorology, and archaeology. New Yorker Michael Frank, who settled in

Southport (Kenosha), lent his talents to newspaper editing, various reform movements, state politics, and the promotion of improved public education. The Pennsylvanian William R. Smith had already held a number of political and military offices when he moved to Wisconsin Territory in 1837. Smith settled in the lead region where he published a promotional book and two volumes of Wisconsin history, helped organize the State Historical Society, aided the organization of the Mineral Point Episcopal Church and the town's Masonic Lodge, served as adjutant general of Wisconsin's militia, helped to organize Wisconsin's Democratic Party, and participated in the first constitutional convention.

Wisconsin's transplanted Yankees soon became "westernized" and contributed considerable talent to the new state. Many brought with them the advantages of higher education and previous political or business experience which they found useful in the West. The Yankees formed a self-conscious element in the population and they often favored political, social and economic relations with others of the same background. Some of the Yankees espoused reforms like anti-slavery and temperance. From their ranks came many land speculators, lawyers, merchants, newspaper editors, town promoters, railroad boosters, and political leaders. The majority of delegates to both constitutional conventions came from New York or New England and for the first quarter century of statehood, as the power of the lead miners waned, such Yankee leaders as Rufus King, Alexander W. Randall, James R. Doolittle, George B. Smith, Timothy O. Howe, Edward V. Whiton, and C. C. Washburn controlled Wisconsin politics.

In the East, entrenched vested interests often prevented ambitious young men from gaining high position in political, business or professional life. Farmers in western New England and New York had begun to turn to dairying, pushing others off the land. To those who were dissatisfied in the East, Wisconsin, with its combination of river highways, fertile soil, healthful climate, and lake port markets, had a special appeal. In contrast to its western neighbors, Wisconsin had both a low debt and low taxes, and the new state offered many desirable land tracts on generous terms. Such advantages continued to lure Yankees to Wisconsin.

Many of the same advantages also attracted foreign immigrants. Wisconsin's liberal election laws appealed to those who had just arrived from Europe. Promoters of the new state were unwilling to leave foreign immigration to chance. In 1852 a state commissioner of immigration, stationed in New York, kept the advantages of Wisconsin constantly before the newcomers. He distributed pamphlets in America and Europe, placed advertisements in the European press and in New York foreign language papers, and talked at length with numerous prospective immigrants. Wisconsin's first official promotion agency lasted only four years, but local promoters, land sellers, and the railroads carried on the work. By the time of the Civil War, from New York to Europe the name of Wisconsin meant unusual opportunity for self betterment.

In Germany, Wisconsin had a special meaning. Persecuted Lutherans from northern Germany came to Wisconsin seeking religious freedom. When the Catholic handicraftsmen of southern Germany faced ruinous competition from new machines, they, too, turned to emigration as an answer to their problem. Many citizens of overpopulated German provinces sought relief by moving to the New World. Some who longed for a unified German nation became disillusioned with their prospects in Europe and decided that Wisconsin might provide a more fertile environment for their nationalism than their homeland. In Wisconsin, wrote an enthusiastic patriot in 1847, Ger-

In a letter to his wife, written in the fall of 1855, Carl Schurz pictured the landscape around Watertown where the family was to settle:

I was astonished at the extent to which this region is cultivated and with what energy people have developed the advantages which the soil offers. Several miles west of Watertown the woods cease to be dense and the openings take the place of the forest. These latter are great open spaces set with trees, orchard-like, the soil of which is mostly without any brush but covered with lovely turf. The openings of Wisconsin can best be likened to the open planted sections which one sees in the parks of London. Between the openings, which are crowned by hills, spread out the succulent meadow lands often enlivened by island-like patches of woods, but often also like valleys of small streams extending for miles between the highlands. These elements of the landscape give the most peaceful, pleasant, prosperous pictures. There is here nothing of the ruggedness which attaches to almost every American beauty spot. This type of region repeats itself in the friendliest variation, except that the openings become lighter and the meadow lands more extensive the farther west one goes; until finally at Columbus the far-spread prairie land lies before you. It is astonishing how very rapidly the building up of the country proceeds here; indeed, how rapidly in some neighborhoods even the log house disappears and the pleasanter frame house or a pretty stone building takes its place.— JOSEPH SCHAFER, ED., *Intimate Letters of Carl Schurz, 1841–1869* (Madison, 1928), 149–150.

mans could have "German schools and universities, German literature and art, German science and philosophy, German courts and assemblies;" in fact, they could have "a German state" in which the German language would flourish and the German spirit rule.

Shiploads of immigrants came to America, and some sought homes in Wisconsin. *From* FRANK LESLIE'S ILLUSTRATED *newspaper, January 12, 1856.*

The Germans brought additional skills to Wisconsin. Their craftsmen included highly trained cabinet-makers, leather-workers, textile makers, bakers, brewers, and carpenters. German teachers introduced educational theories popular in the best European universities and German doctors, schooled in the medical centers of the Continent, contributed to the improvement of the practice and professionalization of medicine in Wisconsin.

The German Forty-Eighters introduced something more to Wisconsin. These nationalistic intellectuals, expatriated because of their participation in an unsuccessful political revolution in 1848, brought political enthusi-

Carl Schurz
SHSW Colls.

asm, anti-clerical thought, and a rich cultural background. Their newspapers circulated anti-clerical propa-
ganda ranging from a mild anti-Catholicism to atheism.
They insisted that religion be consistent with scientific
truths, that supernaturalism be abandoned, and that people should be free to do what they wished on Sundays.
They joined the professions, edited many foreign language newspapers and fostered the development of the
musical talent in the German-American community. Mil-

waukee Forty-Eighters founded the American Turnverein Society, which promoted a combined program of German gymnastics with political and social reform. The political exiles from Germany added an element of dissent to Wisconsin. Their contribution contrasted sharply with the far more common conservatism of Wisconsin's immigrants, including the majority of Germans, but its lasting impact had significance in Wisconsin at a later date.

Most of the Forty-Eighters settled in Wisconsin's only real metropolis, Milwaukee, which in 1850 boasted a population of twenty thousand. No other town in the state approached it in size or importance. In the 1850's Wisconsin was a rural state and agriculture its main economic activity. Most settlers were farmers and wheat quickly be-

Restoration of the first Kindergarten in America, established by Mrs. Carl Schurz in Watertown. *SHSW Colls.*

came their chief crop. As railroads slowly penetrated the region, farmers bought up nearby lands. But farming was in a state of rapid change. Emphasis on a cash crop brought increased dependence on improved transportation facilities to reach a national and even a world market. New and complicated farm machinery made farming more expensive and superficially, at least, more like any other business venture. But differences persisted. Farmers had prejudice against cities, against financial interests, and against manufacturing concerns. They believed a man had a right to own the soil he cultivated. Some of them followed with keen interest the plans of certain congressional politicians to give homesteads to settlers from the national public domain. "Vote-yourself-a-farm-bill," the speculators called it.

Along with Wisconsin farming went trade and industry. Farming meant little if farmers could not sell their products. Some flour millers ground wheat from the neighboring fields, but most Wisconsin wheat went through Milwaukee, where it was processed into flour or shipped east across the lakes. Wisconsin farmers also had an interest in lumbering. Farmers needed lumber for their homes and barns. Many in the pine-land section labored in the lumber camps during the cold winter months. Others helped run the sawmills or raft the lumber down the streams.

Mining, too, continued to be important after statehood was achieved, although an ever-increasing number of miners turned to full-time farming. As the ores proved more difficult to extract, some miners moved on to the California gold fields where their expert knowledge and past experience gave them an unusual advantage over their amateur competitors. With the use of more heavy machinery to bring out the ore and pump the water from the mines, mining became a bigger business requiring more capital investment. More of the lead went east and less through New Orleans after the completion of the Illinois-Michigan Canal in 1848 and the first Wisconsin railroad to reach the Mississippi in 1857. As mining declined in Wisconsin's economy, so did the lead region. Fewer of its leaders held state offices, and the Lake Shore area rapidly outstripped it in population.

WISCONSIN'S PRESIDENTIAL VOTE, 1848–1856		
1848	Lewis Cass (Democrat)	14,924
	Zachary Taylor (Whig)	13,642
	Martin Van Buren (Free Soil)	10,261
1852	Franklin Pierce (Democrat)	33,658
	Winfield Scott (Whig)	22,240
	John P. Hale (Free Soil)	8,842
1856	John C. Fremont (Republican)	66,092
	James Buchanan (Democrat)	52,867
	Millard Fillmore (American)	579

Wisconsin's expanding economic life came to a rapid halt with the Panic of 1857. Drought years had already hit the farmers and the depression added to their heavy indebtedness. Miners were idle. Lumbermen could not sell their logs. Merchants were forced into bankruptcy. Immigration slowed to a virtual standstill. Although they did not close their doors, banks suspended specie payment and credit was nonexistent.

The panic killed what was left of Wisconsin's optimism over a future under statehood. Earlier political failures had exposed the inadequacies of local leadership. Now it seemed that the state could not sufficiently cope with the problems of an expanding economy. In early 1860 Edward G. Ryan expressed the new attitude in an address to the State Historical Society. He said Wisconsin was "Bankrupt in finance, bankrupt in fame and credit, bankrupt in self-respect." Success had replaced honor, and respect went to men of money rather than to those with intellect and integrity. The "paradise of civilization" had become a "paradise of folly and knavery."

Despite the prevailing mood of pessimism, Wisconsinites did not wholly despair for the future. Merchants hoped for more interdependence in order to gain the advantages of a national market. The beginnings of the consolidation of business establishments into larger ones in such areas as mining, lumbering, railroading, meat packing, grain shipping, and river and lake transportation symbolized a change-over from smallness towards bigness in economic life. The east-west line of Wisconsin railroads brought the more remote sections of the state into closer relationship with the rest of the nation, especially with the east coast. With new conditions came new ideas, and in the years ahead some residents of the Badger State began to argue the advantages of a more powerful national government, a government which could unite the nation economically and cope more adequately with the many problems that had not been solved under sovereign statehood.

SUGGESTED ADDITIONAL READING

Beitzinger, Alfons J. *Edward G. Ryan: Lion of the Law* (Madison, 1960).

Byrne, Frank L. "Maine Law Versus Lager Beer: A Dilemma of Wisconsin's Young Republican Party," in the *Wisconsin Magazine of History*, 42:115–120 (Winter, 1958–1959).

Campbell, Henry C. *Wisconsin in Three Centuries, 1634–1905* (4 vols., New York, 1906), III, 29–136.

Clark, James I. *Wisconsin Grows to Statehood: Immigration and Internal Improvements* (Madison, 1955).

————. *Increase A. Lapham: Scientist and Scholar* (Madison, 1957).

————. *Education in Wisconsin* (Madison, 1958).

Hesseltine, William B. "Lyman Copeland Draper, 1815–1891," in the *Wisconsin Magazine of History,* 35:163–166, 231–234 (Spring, 1952).

————. *Pioneer's Mission: The Story of Lyman Copeland Draper* (Madison, 1954).

Holmes, Frederick L. "First Constitutional Convention in Wisconsin, 1846," in *Proceedings of the State Historical Society of Wisconsin,* 1905:227–251.

Jorgenson, Lloyd P. *The Founding of Public Education in Wisconsin* (Madison, 1956).

Kellogg, Louise Phelps. "The Admission of Wisconsin to Statehood," in Milo M. Quaife, ed., *The Movement for Statehood, 1845–1846* (Madison, 1918), 18–29.

Paxson, Frederic L. "Wisconsin—A Constitution of Democracy," in Milo M. Quaife, ed., *The Movement for Statehood, 1845–1846* (Madison, 1918), 30–53.

Quaife, Milo M. *Wisconsin, Its History and Its People, 1634–1924* (4 vols., Chicago, 1924), I, 473–554.

————. "Wisconsin's Saddest Tragedy," in the *Wisconsin Magazine of History,* 5:264–283 (March, 1922).

————, ed. *The Attainment of Statehood* (Madison, 1928).

————. *The Convention of 1846* (Madison, 1919).

————. *The Movement for Statehood, 1845–1846* (Madison, 1918).

————. *The Struggle over Ratification, 1846–1847* (Madison, 1920).

Raney, William Francis. *Wisconsin: A Story of Progress* (New York, 1940), 124–154.

Still, Bayrd. "State-Making in Wisconsin, 1846–48: An Illustration of the Statehood Process," in the *Wisconsin Magazine of History,* 20:34–59 (September, 1936).

Tenney, Horace A., and David Atwood. *Memorial Record of the Fathers of Wisconsin, Containing Sketches of . . . the Members of the Constitutional Conventions of 1846 and 1847–8* (Madison, 1880).

Van Tassel, David D. "William Rudolph Smith, A Cultural Capitalist," in the *Wisconsin Magazine of History*, 36:241–244, 276–280 (Summer, 1953).

Wittke, Carl. "The German Forty-eighters," in O. Fritiof Ander, ed., *The John H. Hauberg Historical Essays* (Rock Island, Illinois, 1954), 41–49.

CHAPTER 4

The Civil War and Its Aftermath 1860–1876

T HE Civil War affected every aspect of life in the Badger State. All individuals, whether or not they became a part of the Northern military effort, felt its repercussions. The war unified the nation politically and Wisconsin, as a state, became increasingly dependent upon the new national government, created under a Republican administration that was keen to turn a temporary partisan advantage into a permanent arrangement. Economically, the war brought prosperity to Wisconsin—a prosperity based upon an increased consolidation of transportation and industrial activity, a growing control of local economic affairs by the national government, and a new dependence upon eastern financial interests and markets. The Civil War marked a turning point in Wisconsin history, but the changes were mostly a culmination or deepening of trends already begun in its formative years.

In the years preceding the Civil War most residents of Wisconsin took little interest in the slavery issue. While the great majority were not proslavery, only a few became ardent antislavery crusaders. A small minority of Wisconsin abolitionists saw every event in terms of a struggle between slavery and freedom, a fight between sin and godliness. It was the old struggle between the forces of darkness and the self-appointed children of light. But slavery was a distant institution and most of Wisconsin's farmers and town dwellers were not inclined to become aroused until it appeared as a direct threat to their own interests in the sectional struggle for control of the national government.

The abolition movement, which began as a moral crusade, became a political issue closely tied in with a number of other objectives. In the 1840's political abolitionists supported the Liberty Party, which in Wisconsin was never strong enough to elect a territorial delegate to Congress. In 1848 the Free Soil Party and its candidate, Martin Van Buren, broadened the appeal from antislavery to include such aims as free homesteads for settlers, low revenue tariff, and federal aid to internal improvements. The party's slavery plank was not abolitionist, but simply opposed any further extension of slavery into the territories. Supported by a coalition of antislavery or "conscience" Whigs, disgruntled Democrats and Liberty Party men, the Van Buren followers used the election slogan "Free soil, free speech, free labor and free men." In Wisconsin the many-sided Free Soil appeal was more successful than in the nation at large. Besides electing Charles Durkee to Congress, the voters sent twenty Free Soilers

WISCONSIN AND THE FUGITIVE SLAVE LAW

Joshua Glover, a laborer in a sawmill near Racine, was arrested as a fugitive slave on March 10, 1854. Sherman M. Booth participated in Glover's rescue and escape from the Milwaukee jail where he was held. In his newspaper, the DAILY FREE DEMOCRAT, Booth published numerous items like the following in which he boasted of Wisconsin's attitude towards the Fugitive Slave Law:

THE FUGITIVE SLAVE LAW REPEALED

We send greetings to the Free States of the Union, that, in Wisconsin, the Fugitive Slave Law is repealed! The first attempt to enforce the law, in this State, has signally, gloriously failed! No Slave-catcher can hereafter tread our soil but at his peril. The Slave Power may repeal the Compromises in favor of Freedom. We will repeal those in favor of Slavery. The Slave Power may pass its Nebraska bills extending Slavery over Free territory, and exclude all foreign-born inhabitants from voting and holding office, even though they have declared their intentions to become citizens. Our foreign-born citizens send back the indignant answer—NO MORE COMPROMISES WITH SLAVERY! FREEDOM IT MUST AND SHALL BE PRESERVED! PERISH ALL ENACTMENTS ESTABLISHING SLAVERY ON FREE SOIL!—Milwaukee DAILY FREE DEMOCRAT, March 13, 1854.

to the state legislature.

The movement against the extension of slavery proved to have a much greater popular appeal than abolition. It gave the people of the North and West a weapon for containing slavery and thereby checking the future growth of

Civil War / 101

Southern power. Both Democratic and Whig politicians hoped that the Compromise of 1850 would permanently remove the slave issue from politics, but the Fugitive Slave Law, a part of the agreement, proved to be very unpopular in the North and kept the agitation alive. Within four years Stephen A. Douglas's Kansas-Nebraska Bill, with its provision for popular sovereignty as the manner of settling the question of slavery in the territories, gave the signal for an even more intense argument over the extension of slavery. The heated debate led directly to the break-up of the existing political parties and added to the rift between the North and the South which soon led to Civil War.

Numerous northern political leaders promoted anti-Nebraska meetings in the early months of 1854, and at such a meeting in Wisconsin the Republican Party was born. Alvan E. Bovay of Ripon, a Whig friend of Horace Greeley, called a meeting late in February to protest the Kansas-Nebraska Bill, then under consideration in Congress. The first meeting, held in the Ripon Congregational Church, was followed by another on March 20 in a frame schoolhouse. At the second meeting representatives of various political groups took a strong stand against the Kansas-Nebraska measure and suggested the formation of a new party to be called Republican. Within a year the young party had state organizations in a number of northern states.

Even before the furor over the Kansas-Nebraska Bill, sympathy for fugitive slaves was common in Wisconsin, and such sentiment grew in strength with the passing of time. Many who would not meddle with the South's peculiar institution would gladly give a runaway slave food and shelter or verbal directions for reaching Canada. Not many fugitives traveled through Wisconsin; a few cases caused a great commotion. The drawn-out legal and political squabbles stemming from abolitionist-editor Sherman M. Booth's assistance to Joshua Glover, a fugitive slave, focused national attention on the rabid reformer and led the Wisconsin Supreme Court to nullify the fed-

Sherman M. Booth
SHSW Colls.

eral Fugitive Slave Law of 1850. In the 1850's, both opposition to the Fugitive Slave Law and the states' rights doctrine of the decision met with the favor of many people in Wisconsin. Booth's martyrdom made good newspaper copy and helped sell many copies of his Milwaukee *Daily Free Democrat*, but it did not convert many of his neighbors to the position of extreme abolitionism which he supported.

The German refugee Carl Schurz was equally unsuccessful in his attempt to win Wisconsin's Germans over to the Republican Party by emphasizing the slave issue. By early 1858 Schurz was convinced that all other issues gave way "before the overwhelming magnitude of the slavery question." He also admitted that he was then "more popular among the Americans than among the Germans" whom he was supposed to convert. Some of his compatriots suspected in him a strong thirst for power; others simply were not moved by what Schurz believed to be the great question of the day. Few people in Wisconsin were. Despite Carl Schurz's claim that the Republican victory of 1860 was his fight, it was neither Schurz nor his issues that carried the state for Lincoln.

When William H. Seward and a group of prominent Republicans toured Wisconsin in September of 1860, they emphasized the issues that would count most with the voters. Speaking in Madison, Seward promised that a Republican victory would bring a homestead act for the farmers and federal aid for much desired internal improvements. Throughout the state local Republicans repeatedly promised railroads and other improvements. No Westerner quarreled with the need for such facilities but Wisconsin residents wanted to be sure that any internal improvements would benefit Wisconsin rather than Illinois or other nearby areas.

There was good reason for concern. Even before Congress had made any land grants to Wisconsin railroads, the Rock River Valley Union Railroad, a proposed north-south road to run from southern Wisconsin to some point on Lake Superior, requested federal aid. Despite the political influence of A. Hyatt Smith, a Janesville Democrat who was president of the company, the road's bid for a land grant brought no results. The defeat was caused in part by Democratic factional feuds, and in part by the

South Carolina secedes!
SHSW Colls.

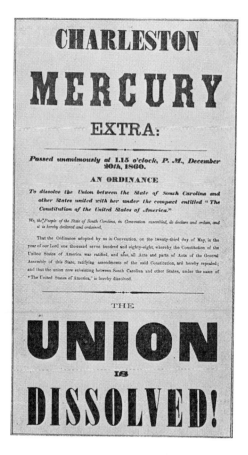

CHARLESTON

MERCURY

EXTRA:

Passed unanimously at 1.15 o'clock, P. M., December 20th, 1860.

AN ORDINANCE

To dissolve the Union between the State of South Carolina and other States united with her under the compact entitled "The Constitution of the United States of America."

We, the People of the State of South Carolina, in Convention assembled, do declare and ordain, and it is hereby declared and ordained,

That the Ordinance adopted by us in Convention, on the twenty-third day of May, in the year of our Lord one thousand seven hundred and eighty-eight, whereby the Constitution of the United States of America was ratified, and also, all Acts and parts of Acts of the General Assembly of this State, ratifying amendments of the said Constitution, are hereby repealed; and that the union now subsisting between South Carolina and other States, under the name of "The United States of America," is hereby dissolved.

THE

UNION

IS

DISSOLVED!

fear of many that such a road would harm the state by diverting traffic away from Milwaukee to Chicago. Shortly afterwards, the Chicago, St. Paul and Fond du Lac Railroad took over the Valley Road and made another unsuccessful effort to obtain a land grant. The Wisconsin road proposed to connect with Stephen A. Douglas's Illinois Central at Chicago and lead south through Illinois. It was to be part of a great railroad chain paralleling the Mississippi River and helping to bind the North and South together. But it was not until years after the Civil War that a Wisconsin railroad actually reached Lake Superior; the roads ran east-west rather than north-south and their direction helped seal the state's economic destiny. The new roads enabled lumbermen and farmers to send products to the area being rapidly settled west of the Mississippi. In the other direction, they carried Wisconsin products to New York and other eastern ports rather than to New Orleans.

The outbreak of war in April, 1861, assured a strengthening of relations between the West and the East. The increased volume of eastward-moving trade, along with wartime economic developments, guaranteed Milwaukee's strategic position both as a port city and as a manufacturing center. The closing of the lower Mississippi River settled the matter. Whether Wisconsin products should be shipped through New Orleans or the Atlantic ports was no longer open for discussion. The new and hastily-constructed railroads running across the state were overwhelmed with more business than their wildest promoters had dreamed might come their way—more business, in fact, than they could effectively handle. Freight rates skyrocketed, and went even higher when ice closed the Great Lakes. During the boom period the railroads reaped huge profits and many Wisconsin farmers and businessmen began to curse the profiteering practices of the same roads whose construction they had hopefully helped to finance only a few years earlier.

When the war began Wisconsin quickly rallied to support the Union cause. Republican Governor Alexander Randall was willing, even anxious, to pledge the state's entire resources to the war effort. Governor Randall objected to what he believed to be the slow motion of the Lincoln administration in dealing with secession. When the government in Washington requested one Wisconsin regiment, Randall recruited several and demanded that they be put to good use. The governor excoriated the South. At a conference of western governors in Cleveland in May, 1861, he said the Union Army "should blaze a broad track through the whole South, . . . [wiping] out not only traitors, but the seed of traitors." With each regiment the zealous war governor also sent an agent of the state who was to look after the health and needs of the soldiers. Despite Democratic jeering at Governor Randall's "wet nurse" system, Wisconsin's three other Civil War governors continued the practice.

Many Wisconsin residents shared their governor's enthusiasm for the war. In its early days, at least, volunteers were plentiful. Not all of those who joined the colors were as vindictive as Randall but signed up for many reasons. A very few, like Chauncey Cooke of Buffalo County, fought to end slavery. Many more believed they were called upon to preserve the Union. Most, however, had personal reasons that were far more important to them than any national war aims. Some wanted to get away from home, and not a few hoped to make political uses of a wartime record. Of the many who hoped to advance themselves in the army ranks only a few succeeded. Among them was Brigadier-General Edward Bragg, who early confided to his wife, "as I have to stay in the service, I fight for 'a star' or a coffin."

A recruiting poster
SHSW Colls.

Contemporary sketch of Camp Randall
SHSW Colls.

Wisconsin's soldiers fought in every major battle of the Civil War. Before the end of the conflict more than 91,000 men from the Badger State served in the Union ranks, for terms ranging from three months to three years. Wisconsin furnished fifty-six regiments, with many of their members re-enlisting two or more times. Recruits were trained at Milwaukee, Fond du Lac, Racine, and Madison, where the converted fairgrounds of the state agricultural society became Camp Randall, Wisconsin's major Civil War training place. Camp Randall also housed Confederate prisoners of war, some of whom died and were buried there.

The Iron Brigade, commanded at various times by Milwaukee editor Rufus King, Lucius Fairchild, and Edward S. Bragg, and composed of the 2nd, 6th, and 7th Wisconsin Volunteers, plus the 19th Indiana and the 24th Michigan, was Wisconsin's most famous Civil War fighting unit. The Iron Brigade fought in the Army of the Potomac and suffered unusually heavy casualties at Gainesville, Antietam, and Gettysburg. Some of the Wisconsin regiments were composed mostly of various nationality groups: the 9th, 26th, 27th and 45th were Germans, the 15th Norwegians, and the 17th Irish. The 8th Wisconsin became the "Eagle Regiment" because of "Old Abe," a pet bald eagle which it carried into battle on a perch proudly flying the American flag.

Wisconsin men distinguished themselves in numerous battles and skirmishes. At Williamsburg a bayonet charge by the men of the 5th Wisconsin turned the battle into a Union victory. The 2nd Wisconsin cavalry, organized and led by Cadwallader C. Washburn, fought valiantly in western battles at Vicksburg, and in Louisiana, Texas, and Arkansas. Sometimes their Wisconsin experience enabled the men to offer special skills to the Union military

A group from the 7th Wisconsin Volunteers

SHSW Colls.

A guard flag carried by Wisconsin troops
SHSW Colls.

"Old Abe," the War Eagle

Battle of Chickamauga
SHSW Colls.

effort. In the spring of 1864 Colonel Joseph Bailey saved a fleet of Union gunboats and transports stranded in the Red River of Louisiana. To accomplish the feat, Bailey and several thousand lumberjacks from the 23rd and 24th regiments used a technique for damming and deepening the river that they had learned in Wisconsin's lumber camps.

Besides fighting to preserve the Union, Wisconsin soldiers also helped to put down the Sioux Indians of Minnesota who revolted against white domination in 1862. After killing about five hundred settlers the Minnesota Indians were defeated and thirty-eight of them executed. In Wisconsin news of the Sioux uprising caused a nightmarish scare among the people. Although there was no danger of an Indian rebellion, Governor Edward Salomon requested federal troops. In Superior all able-bodied males between the ages of eighteen and sixty were required to

Unloading supplies for the Union Army at City Point, Va. *Library of Congress Photo.*

report for guard duty, and in the eastern and southern parts of the state settlers in outlying districts fled in panic to the nearest large town. Rumors of mass murders and sacked towns spread like prairie fire until the people, realizing that the danger was imaginary, returned to the business of fighting the Civil War or supplying the equipment and supplies necessary for the war.

Wisconsin soldiers had varying experiences while serving in the Union Army. Chauncey Cooke was so young he had to lie about his age in order to enlist. Private Cooke of the 25th Regiment was first sent to Minnesota in the Sioux campaign, then to Camp Randall for drill and several months of tedious waiting, followed by a transfer to Columbus, Kentucky, where he was mostly involved in guarding Confederate prisoners. In the summer of 1863 Cooke participated in the fighting around Vicksburg, then went to Helena, Arkansas, for guard duty. Later he contracted pneumonia and was hospitalized in Memphis. After recovering he joined his regiment in time to take part in the bitter fighting which Sherman's army encountered as the troops inched southward through Georgia. Before they reached Atlanta, Cooke was granted a furlough and then sent to Camp Randall for the duration of the war. For Cooke, as well as for many others, the fighting was interspersed with guard duty, drill, hospitalization, times of fun, and long periods of seemingly endless waiting.

Many of the Wisconsin youth who marched against the South did not return. Nearly twelve thousand died from battle wounds or disease in army camps. Thousands more

A field post office

were wounded. When word reached Madison of the heavy casualties at Shiloh, Governor Louis P. Harvey collected supplies for the wounded and set out to visit the Wisconsin men among them. After accomplishing his mission he lost his life by drowning when he attempted to step from one steamboat to another in the Tennessee River. Mrs. Cordelia Harvey, his widow, organized charitable activities for wounded soldiers, and arranged transfers for many of them to Northern hospitals. Toward the end of the war Mrs. Harvey founded an orphanage in Madison for the children of Wisconsin's soldiers who were killed in service.

At the same time that Wisconsin soldiers fought for various reasons, the people back home, too, held different attitudes towards the war. Not all agreed that it was necessary to fight the South at all, while many objected to the abridgment of civil liberties and other unconstitutional measures of the Lincoln administration. In Illinois Governor Richard Yates waxed hysterical about alleged "copperhead" threats, and so did Governor Oliver Morton of Indiana. Some extremist Republican editors in the Badger State also detected a nest of copperheads in their midst. There was very little basis for such a scare. The majority of the opposition party were War Democrats who objected to Lincoln's unconstitutional acts, but agreed that the war should be fought to a victorious finish.

Most of Wisconsin's German population remained loyal to the Democrats and critical of the administration's conduct of the war. Peter Victor Deuster, editor and publisher of the pro-Catholic, Democratic Milwaukee *Seebote,* became a leading spokesman for the Wisconsin Germans who opposed the government's war policies. Deuster's newspaper gained a large audience of German-speaking readers and did much to counteract the influence of Carl Schurz and some of the other pro-Republican

Carl Schurz in uniform
SHSW Colls.

Forty-eighters. Some of the Wisconsin Germans carried their opposition further and objected to fighting in "Mr. Lincoln's War." The Germans in Washington, Ozaukee, and Milwaukee counties participated in a series of anti-draft demonstrations in 1862, but even these disturbances were considerably milder and less serious than similar outbursts in New York and some other sections of the nation.

A much more serious political threat was Edward G. Ryan's speech to Milwaukee Democrats in September of 1862. The Republicans labeled the address the "Bible of Copperheadism," but it was more an attack on the Lincoln administration than a criticism of the war. Ryan excoriated both the Southern secessionists and the Northern abolitionists. He denounced the revolt as "unnecessary, unjustifiable," and "unholy." He insisted that the war should "be carried on by the government *for* the constitution alone, and *under* the constitution alone." He criticized the administration for infractions of the constitution including the suspension of the writ of *habeas corpus,* the military arrests of civilians, and the suppression of opposition newspapers. Democratic printers quickly published Ryan's powerful address in a pamphlet. Within a month they had distributed more than 100,000 copies in both German and English, and in Democratic Milwaukee the strong arguments fell on fertile ground.

Ryan's moderation was in marked contrast to the utterances of Marcus M. "Brick" Pomeroy, editor of the La Crosse *Democrat* and the most extreme of all the "copperhead" editors. Pomeroy grew increasingly critical as the war progressed, advancing from a position of calm opposition to bitter vituperation. Firsthand observation of the horrors of war and the profiteering, political favoritism, and fraud which accompanied it turned Pomeroy into a fanatical crusader whose venom-dipped pen stopped at nothing. In the spring of 1863 he told his readers that without the chance to make political uses of the war and to steal Southern cotton, the war would end; "were there no rich speculators and moneyed men, as selfish and unprincipled as the devil himself, now controlling this crusade, there would be peace over the land today." The La Crosse editor also appealed to sectional prejudice, claiming that the war was making the West the "slave and servant of New England." During the presidential campaign of 1864 he labelled Lincoln "The Widow-Maker of the 19th Century." Pomeroy later regretted that he added, "and if he is elected to misgovern for another four years, we trust some bold hand will pierce his heart with dagger point for the public good."

Although many Wisconsin Germans and residents of strong pro-Democratic regions paid close heed to the words of Ryan and Pomeroy, most of the state's voters continued to support the Republican cause. Republicanism was both patriotic and profitable during the Civil War. The Panic of 1857 and its aftermath of severe depression contributed substantially to the Republican victory of 1860. The secession crisis touched off another brief financial upset, but the war that followed brought quick economic recovery. Although the West, as a growing agricultural section, had been hit less hard by the depression than the East, Western bankers, merchants, farmers, and lumbermen were all anxious for better times. The war provided new business opportunities for all elements of the working population and also accelerated economic changes already begun.

The upper Mississippi and the Great Lakes once again became the scene of a great transportation boom. Vessels that had been partially dismantled were put back into service and unemployed sailors found work plentiful. Along with the new wartime boom came combination. The independently-owned river vessel became a thing of the past, and more and more business fell into the hands of two or three large companies. By 1863 Captain W. F. Davidson's La Crosse and St. Paul Packet Company virtually monopolized trade on the upper Mississippi. Davidson bought out his only competitor and in 1866 when the arrangement was made public his company, reorganized as the Northwestern Packet Company, owned $1,500,000 worth of property including steamboats, barges, dockyards, and 15,000 acres of woodland.

The monopolization of lake transportation was more complicated than that of river transportation. No one company gained control of all the lake traffic. However, lake boats carried huge quantities of grain eastward. Milwaukee outstripped Chicago as a wheat port and became the world's greatest primary wheat market. In both cities grain was inspected, weighed, and graded at the huge elevators which were often owned by the railroads. Wheat shippers had a choice between the railroad or the lake vessels, and the slower moving sailing craft were rapidly losing out to the larger and faster steam vessels. Many of the lake steamers were owned by the larger railroad companies. Wheat farmers and shippers protested the growing trend towards monopoly, but their protests had little effect during the war when wheat brought good prices at the port cities.

The threat of railroad monopoly was more real. The same railroads which Wisconsin residents had assumed would solve most of their problems became the object of their wrath when such unrealistic hopes proved false. When the war came, railroads served most communities in the southern, settled sections of Wisconsin. The roads recovered from the depression but ended up in the hands of a few large companies. Roads which builders had hastily constructed to serve a sparsely-populated area soon found themselves swamped with business. Competitive rate wars with steamship lines often ended in rate agreements. More and more the railroads owned the lake vessels too. Rates soared and once more protests in the war years had virtually no results. A few interests controlled all the Wisconsin roads, and there was little that the dependent farmers could do about it.

In one area, however, the Wisconsin farmers won a battle against the railroads. With new prosperity came renewed demands for paying those who had mortgaged their homes and farms to help build the railroads. The Grand State League, a pressure group, championed the farmers' cause and made it a political issue in the state. A. M. Thomson, editor of the Hartford *Home League*, urged the mortgagors to keep the single issue constantly in mind. In April, 1861, Thomson told Wisconsin's farm mortgagors that "whether Pickens or Sumter is or is not evacuated—whether Huston or Wigfall is in the ascendant in Texas—whether there is polygamy in Utah or idolatry in Boolah-boolah-Gah, should be matters of secondary importance to them." The issue got attention; between 1858 and 1863 Wisconsin legislators passed fourteen different laws providing some kind of relief to the farm mortgage group. Most of the laws were either nullified by the courts or were never enforced, but nevertheless the roads came to terms with their debtors. Some companies gave farmers liberal terms to retire their farm mortgages. Part of the land grant of 1856 was used to pay the farmers. The railroad boards of directors were more careful and honest in future dealings with their Wisconsin patrons.

Good crop prices mitigated the wrath of Wisconsin farmers during the Civil War boom. "Wheat is king," announced the Milwaukee *Sentinel,* "and Wisconsin is the center of the Empire." In spite of some fluctuations in prices and weather, the war years were good ones for the farmers. Wheat continued to be the main crop and its production became increasingly mechanized. When young men left the farms for the battlefields they were replaced by machinery as well as by women and children. Wisconsin farmers put thousands of mechanical reapers, threshers, harrows, and other farm machines to use. The wheat shipped eastward as grain or flour helped feed the loyal states and Europe.

Although wheat was king, there were competitors. Wisconsin farmers tried to produce nearly everything for which there was a known demand. They grew corn, oats, rye, and barley to supply local needs. They raised sheep to furnish wool for the government. They had little success with sorghum and sugar cane, but did much better with sugar beets and tobacco. Towards the close of the war they devoted considerable time and energy to raising hops, but the profitable craze lasted only a few years. Another trend that began about the same time had more lasting results. More and more farmers added dairying to their activities and in 1864 Chester Hazen of Fond du Lac County built the state's first cheese factory. In the years to follow, agricultural journals advised Badger farmers to "substitute the cow for the plow" and there were those who profited from the advice.

Lumbering, too, changed during the Civil War years. Wisconsin's rich pineries were hardly touched before 1860, and the effects of the depression did not leave the lumber industry until late in 1862. But recovery was thorough and in the next few years there was an unprecedented demand for lumber, both in the growing section to the west of the Mississippi, and in the East. Lumbering became a big business with larger lumber camps, the introduction of huge log rafts on the rivers and the lakes, the booming and improvement companies, the steam sawmill and the circular saw. Each year more Wisconsin lumber left the state as logs to be manufactured into wood products in the western Mississippi towns or in Chicago.

Lumbermen, although they still employed some wasteful methods, began to use sawdust for fuel and to make lath and pickets from slabs, and shingles from culls. The manufacturing of wood products, especially shingles, became an important Wisconsin industry. During the war the skilled shingle maker, who had often combined his trade with farming, gave way to machine production of shingles, and the center of the industry shifted from Manitowoc to Green Bay.

Other Wisconsin industries also started or developed during the early 1860's. In Milwaukee meatpacking and tanning expanded rapidly. Milwaukee breweries supplied beer to the Germans and others who learned to like it during the war when the government placed a heavy tax on stronger drinks. Milwaukee's numerous shops and small factories also employed many skilled printers, cigarmakers, coopers, joiners, tailors, carpenters, and ship caulkers. Some of the craftsmen organized into unions, but they were more like fraternal organizations than modern pressure groups. Intimate employer-employee relationships, a strong sense of individual pride as craftsmen, and continued replacement of workers with machines all worked against the development of a political labor movement.

Wisconsin industry grew throughout the war years, but agriculture remained the basic activity, employing five-sixths of the population. Some of the new industries were closely related to farming. Milwaukee flour mills depended on the Wisconsin wheat crop and its breweries used the hops which many of the state's farmers raised. In turn the small but important iron industry in Milwaukee furnished raw iron for factories which manufactured farm machinery. One of them, the J. I. Case factory in Racine, soon became one of the largest producers of threshing machines in the region. Wisconsin's industries gradually served a larger market than just the state; in some cases, like flour milling, the market even became national.

A number of the new industries required ore, and mining in the lead region enjoyed a profitable revival. Large eastern firms purchased some of the worked-over mines and resumed operations with the use of heavy, expensive machinery to drain the water and to dig deeper. The needs of war put a premium on lead and the price soared. Some of the older mines proved to be far from depleted, but after several additional years of mining even the new machinery could no longer make the diggings profitable. Lead region miners also mined zinc, which earlier had been looked upon as waste, but was vital to the Civil War arms industry.

Two other new mining interests proved unprofitable. There was much peat in Wisconsin but those who invested in the cutting and processing of it soon learned that it was not of sufficiently good quality to pay for its processing as a fuel. A short-lived petroleum boom in 1865 had an even less substantial basis. Unscrupulous promoters and bogus geologists were partly to blame for the waste of time and capital in undertakings destined to fail for the lack of petroleum. The false boom was more a symptom of a national phenomenon than a legitimate economic endeavor.

All of these expanded economic activities, sound or unsound, required financing by Wisconsin's banks. No other interests were changed more drastically by the war than banking. Although Wisconsin bankers weathered the Panic of 1857, they were seriously hit by secession. Notes of Wisconsin banks were backed up by state securities deposited with the bank comptroller, and many of these securities were from southern states. Additional trouble stemmed from the banks' practice of issuing far more notes than they could possibly redeem. Milwaukee's Alexander Mitchell (the grandfather of the famous Billy Mitchell) working through the conservative Wisconsin Bankers Association, led a movement which forced many of the unsound banks to fail. In the process, workers who had been paid in worthless bank notes rioted and troops put down the disturbances. Eventually Mitchell and the bankers bought up a large war loan and used the state bonds to back up their notes, retiring the Southern securities. The state gave generous terms and the banks found the procedure a profitable one. By the fall of 1861 Wisconsin banks were in a sound condition and their notes helped finance the state's expanded financial activities.

Notes of state-chartered banks, however, still varied in value, and Secretary of the Treasury Salmon P. Chase worked out a program for national control of banking. The first National Bank Act of 1863 was not coercive, and only a few Wisconsin banks joined the National Bank system until a new law in 1865 virtually taxed state bank notes out of existence. Emergency state legislation protected the Wisconsin bank notes, but eventually they had to give way to the new national bank notes. Within a year after the close of the war, Wisconsin currency ceased to circulate and all notes were retired. National control of banking and currency was one of the results of the war.

Increased national aid to education was another. From its beginning the Civil War affected education in Wisconsin as in other states. The public schools which had been hard hit by the economic depression quickly recovered with the war prosperity, but the University suffered a temporary setback. Both faculty members and students joined the ranks. The University Light Guards became the University Myrmidons in 1863. Before the war ended more than two hundred students and others connected with the University took up arms, most for the Union cause, a few for the Southern Confederacy. In 1864 all but one graduate enlisted; there was no commencement that year. By 1865 the University was back to normal size with 306 students and a new source of income. The Agricultural College Act of 1862 gave Wisconsin a land grant, which the legislature accepted for the University. In return, the University agreed to include agricultural and military subjects in its offerings. In 1866 the University was completely reorganized and the following year the legislature gave it financial support for the first time. The new income gave new life to the institution and helped lay a basis for a much greater future.

Aid to education was a concrete example of Republican benevolent policy, and as such it added strength to the national political party. Before the Civil War the Republicans had no national organization. State and local committees ran the party. It was a coalition party composed of former Whigs, anti-Nebraska Democrats, Free Soilers, abolitionists, and other reformers. The Democrats jeeringly called the party "Old Fusion." In 1860 the Republican platform had offered something for nearly every group in the Northern population. It promised free homesteads to Western settlers, federal aid to promoters of a Pacific railroad, a high protective tariff to manufacturers and factory workers, and for industrialists needing cheap labor there was to be a relaxation of the immigration laws. The one cohesive element in the campaign was the insistence that no additional territory be opened to slavery.

TERMS OF WISCONSIN'S GOVERNORS, 1858–1878

January, 1858–1862	Alexander W. Randall (Republican)
January–April, 1862	Louis P. Harvey (Republican) *
April, 1862–1864	Edward Salomon (Republican)
January, 1864–1866	James T. Lewis (Republican)
January, 1866–1872	Lucius Fairchild (Republican)
January, 1872–1874	Cadwallader C. Washburn (Republican)
January, 1874–1876	William R. Taylor (Democratic-Liberal-Reform)
January, 1876–1878	Harrison Ludington (Republican)

—WISCONSIN BLUE BOOK, 1915 (Madison, 1915), 367.

* After serving in office seventy-three days, Governor Harvey was drowned in an accident in Tennessee and Edward Salomon, the lieutenant governor, filled out his term.

The Republican victory of 1860 was the triumph of a new party with many aspiring leaders. The state governors headed the local machines and carried their states for Lincoln. Yet by the end of the war Lincoln was clearly the leader of the party and the important decisions came from Washington, rather than from the various states. As the country itself was unified through war, the Republican Party was also nationalized. In 1860 the local bosses and state governors led the party; by 1865 they had been absorbed into the national machine. The state machines, however, continued to play an important role within the national party structure.

During the Civil War and in the years immediately following it, Boss Elisha W. Keyes of Madison headed the political group known as the "Madison Regency" which dominated the Wisconsin Republican organization. As Madison's mayor and postmaster, Keyes and his friends made use of the patronage to control the party. Keyes handpicked candidates, manipulated conventions, directed the course of the state legislature, and suggested men for federal posts. Within a few years the new Republican administration rested on as efficient a national political machine as the Democrats had devised under Jackson and his successors. But along with Republican efficiency went both graft and corruption which eventually contributed to the party's downfall.

In the war years Republican prosperity was a main attraction of the party. One by one the various platform promises of 1860 were fulfilled. The federal government doled out money for railroad construction, other internal improvements, and higher education. The Republican Congress passed a homestead law, raised the tariff, relaxed immigration laws, and provided for a national banking system. The Republicans also capitalized on wartime patriotism and equated loyalty to the Union with loyalty to

Elisha W. Keyes
SHSW Colls.

the administration. The war itself added new assets to the party. Republican politicians became generals and lucrative war contracts often went to party henchmen.

In Wisconsin, however, there was continued competition from the Democrats. Its largest city remained the nation's "Banner Democratic City" throughout the conflict. Republicans did not even nominate candidates in several of Milwaukee's municipal elections. In 1861 Louis P. Harvey ran for governor on both the Republican and Union party tickets. The use of the Union issue helped elect Harvey, but the Democrats were not all willing to be caught again in a trap "where the Republican cat was well concealed under the Union meal." The following year soldier votes and gerrymandering narrowly

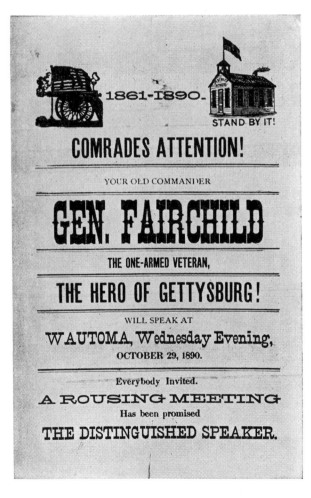

Poster announcing a Fairchild rally
SHSW Colls.

opposite page:
General Lucius Fairchild
SHSW Colls.

saved the state for the Republicans. Even with such tactics three of Wisconsin's five congressmen were Democrats.

After the war Wisconsin Republicans continued to make good use of war hatreds and passions. The Grand Army of the Republic rallied veterans around the flag of General Lucius Fairchild. The general's "empty sleeve," a grim reminder of his heroism at Gettysburg, made him an especially useful candidate. Fairchild served three terms as Wisconsin's governor. Party leaders recognized his peculiar asset, but Fairchild eventually broke with Boss Keyes and the Madison regency. In 1870 Keyes feared that the general was "marshalling his *Grand army*, his *poor* and his *lame* and halt and blind," for a fourth term nomination.

Fairchild made a strong fight but without the support of the party machine he lost the nomination. And he did not rely solely on the "Grand army" for support. Neither had his earlier successes been entirely dependent upon waving the "empty sleeve." As early as 1869 Wisconsin Republicans had been exposed in incidents involving political corruption, and in an effort to cover the sordid revelations, Fairchild had aroused new hopes for federal aid to internal improvements. Large numbers of settlers were moving into the northern half of the state, and the need for improved transportation facilities was becoming increasingly apparent. Fairchild reminded them that a "Republican governor can do much more in such directions with a Republican congress than can a Democratic one." The counties most in need of improvements contributed heavily to Fairchild's re-election.

The internal improvement issue was probably the main one keeping Wisconsin loyally Republican after the war. Westerners supported the high tariffs demanded by the East, and got internal improvements in return. Political leaders from both sections agreed to keep the South in a subordinate position until it, too, was safely Republican. Year after year the uneasy alliance between the West and East was maintained until the 1870's when some Westerners again became convinced that they were being exploited by Eastern financial interests.

The changed attitude was in part a reflection of the experiences of Wisconsin's carpetbaggers, many of whom had gone to the South seeking a new frontier area. Some of the same people who had migrated to frontier Wisconsin saw new political and economic opportunities in the postwar South. The South had rich resources for agriculture and industry and only awaited a Yankee migration to transform it into a wealthy and progressive region. Those who migrated south from Wisconsin included adventurers, businessmen, restless young men including some Civil War veterans, idealists, despots, and office seekers. Former Governor Leonard J. Farwell became a land promoter in postwar Missouri, attracting immigrants there

G.A.R. reunion at Camp Randall

SHSW Colls.

just as he had earlier done in Wisconsin. Milwaukee businessman Lewis J. Higby migrated to New Orleans where he worked to develop its commercial resources. Some of Wisconsin's carpetbaggers were politicians who became involved in the graft and corruption which characterized so much postwar politics in the South as in the rest of the nation.

The opportunities which appealed to various Wisconsin carpetbaggers evaporated by the 1870's. By then it was apparent that the mass migration required to fully develop the South's various resources would not take place. Instead of finding wealth and status the transplanted Northerners sometimes lost what money they had invested and met with social ostracism from the local inhabitants. They were thoroughly disillusioned. The native Southerners gradually regained political control of the region. Furthermore, frontiers in the Far West had a greater attraction for many adventurers than the South. And in Wisconsin a majority of the people found Wisconsin itself to be their most desirable frontier. The continued economic development of the state made possible the utilization of all the intelligence, talent, labor, and capital that might be available. But in order to further the process of Wisconsin's development it was necessary to turn its people's attention away from the South and towards its own problems. Wisconsin politicians also had to accommodate their program to the new situation.

Politically, things came to a head in the state in 1873. The Republican Party, glutted with spoils and drunk with power, was already split into a number of factions. Several elements contributed to the change. War hatreds had worn thin. Senator Matthew H. "Matt" Carpenter was publicly discredited as a shameless defender of the corrupt spoils system. During Governor Cadwallader C. Washburn's administration, Wisconsin Republicans an-

1860	Abraham Lincoln (Republican)	86,110
	Stephen A. Douglas (Democrat)	65,021
	John C. Breckenridge (Southern Dem.)	889
	John Bell (Constitutional Union)	151
1864	Abraham Lincoln (Republican)	68,750
	George B. McClellan (Democrat)	61,839
1868	Ulysses S. Grant (Republican)	108,857
	Horatio Seymour (Democrat)	84,710
1872	Ulysses S. Grant (Republican)	104,992
	Horace Greeley (Dem., Liberal Rep.)	86,477
	Charles O'Conor (Democrat)	834
1876	Rutherford B. Hayes (Republican)	130,070
	Samuel J. Tilden (Democrat)	123,930
	Peter Cooper (Greenback)	1,509
	Green Clay Smith (Prohibition)	27

tagonized many Germans with their support of the unpopular Graham Liquor Law which attempted to regulate closely the sale of liquor. Washburn's veto of a bill authorizing the construction of a bridge across the Mississippi alienated railroad promoters. A new economic depression deflated the optimistic dream of perpetual prosperity. The Democrats seized the opportunity to unite anti-monopolists, Grangers, the liquor and railroad interests, Liberal Republicans, and various reform groups to support William R. Taylor who ran on a People's Reform ticket. The voters elected Taylor along with a Democratic legislature. Taylor served only one term, but in 1874 the reformers elected three congressmen and in 1875 they carried the entire state ticket except for the governorship. The Democratic-Reform coalition, however, failed to hold together, and Wisconsin returned to the Republican camp in 1876.

The America of 1876 was vastly different from that of 1860. Wisconsin, like other states, had been transformed in the process of national consolidation by armed conflict. Nationally-co-ordinated military effort brought national control to an unprecedented degree. Subsidies and grants from the federal treasury brought more conditions and restrictions. The temporary postwar alliance between the East and the West against the South did not prove as useful to the West as many had supposed it would. The Republicans who had made so much capital of Democratic corruption had themselves yielded to the temptations which accompany a long term of power. Wisconsin's reactions to these and other developments within her borders and within the new nation would give, in the years ahead, a new meaning to the state.

SUGGESTED ADDITIONAL READING

Beitzinger, Alfons J. *Edward G. Ryan: Lion of the Law* (Madison, 1960).

————. "The Father of Copperheadism in Wisconsin," in the *Wisconsin Magazine of History*, 39:17–25 (Autumn, 1955).

Campbell, Henry C. *Wisconsin in Three Centuries, 1634–1905* (4 vols., New York, 1906), III, 139–328.

Clark, James I. *The Civil War of Private Cooke: A Wisconsin Boy in the Union Army* (Madison, 1955).

————. *Wisconsin Defies the Fugitive Slave Law: The Case of Sherman M. Booth* (Madison, 1955).

Fish, Carl Russell. "Phases of Economic History of Wisconsin, 1860–70," in *Proceedings of the State Historical Society of Wisconsin*, 1907:204–216.

Hesseltine, William B. *Lincoln's Problems in Wisconsin* (Madison, 1952).

Jorgenson, Lloyd P. *The Founding of Public Education in Wisconsin* (Madison, 1956).

Kaiser, Leo M., ed. "Civil War Letters of Charles W. Carr of the 21st Wisconsin Volunteers," in the *Wisconsin Magazine of History*, 43:264–272 (Summer, 1960).

Klement, Frank. " 'Brick' Pomeroy: Copperhead and Curmudgeon," in the *Wisconsin Magazine of History*, 35:106–113, 156–157 (Winter, 1951).

————. "Copperheads and Copperheadism in Wisconsin: Democratic Opposition to the Lincoln Administration," in the *Wisconsin Magazine of History*, 42:182–188 (Spring, 1959).

————. *The Copperheads in the Middle West* (Chicago, 1960).

————. "The Soldier Vote in Wisconsin During the Civil War," in the *Wisconsin Magazine of History*, 28:37–47 (September, 1944).

Krueger, Leonard B. *History of Commercial Banking in Wisconsin* (Madison, 1933).

Merk, Frederick. *Economic History of Wisconsin During the Civil War Decade* (Madison, 1916).

Oliver, John W. "Draft Riots in Wisconsin During the Civil War," in the *Wisconsin Magazine of History*, 2:334–336 (March, 1919).

Overy, David H., Jr. "The Wisconsin Carpetbaggers: A Group Portrait," in the *Wisconsin Magazine of History*, 44:15–49 (Autumn, 1960).

————. *Wisconsin Carpetbaggers in Dixie* (Madison, 1961).

Quaife, Milo M. *Wisconsin, Its History and Its People, 1634–1924* (4 vols., Chicago, 1924), I, 555–602.

Raney, William Francis. *Wisconsin: A Story of Progress* (New York, 1940), 179–254, 262–280.

Schafer, Joseph. *Carl Schurz: Militant Liberal* (Evansville, Wisconsin, 1930).

————, ed. and translator. *Intimate Letters of Carl Schurz, 1841–1869* (Madison, 1928).

Thompson, E. Bruce. *Matthew Hale Carpenter: Webster of the West* (Madison, 1954).

Williams, Helen J. and Harry. "Wisconsin Republicans and Reconstruction, 1865–70," in the *Wisconsin Magazine of History*, 23:17–39 (September, 1939).

Civil War / 135

CHAPTER 5

Wisconsin in the New Nation
1876–1900

T HE Civil War completed the process of national unifi-
cation in the United States, a process which was more than
political in its scope. True, in the conflict the several states
lost nearly all their claim to sovereignty and emerged in a
clearly subordinate position to the national government.
The war also brought economic changes to America. Indeed, the transformation touched upon every area of life.
From the ashes of the nation's biggest and most costly war
there emerged a pattern of bigness in both business and
government. With each passing year a larger percentage
of the population congregated into cities, where commerce
and industry demanded the skill and labor of hundreds of
thousands of Wisconsin's workers. Farmers, too, were becoming increasingly dependent upon new and impersonal
forces largely beyond their control—the railroads, the

factories producing new, expensive farm machinery, and market conditions in distant parts of the nation and even of the globe.

The people of Wisconsin shared in the changes taking place in the nation, but not all of the events in the state's history from 1876 to 1900 were merely a reflection of outside developments. Within the framework of a rapidly changing nation Wisconsin's people continued to exploit the natural resources of the area and contributed substantially to the further economic development of the entire nation.

The last quarter of the nineteenth century was a time of continued growth for the state. Thousands of immigrants came to work the farms, build the railroads, construct the city buildings, and cut and manufacture into finished

Early sawmill, Unity

H. H. Bennett Studios—SHSW Colls.

Logging crews vied to haul the largest load. *SHSW Colls.*

products the trees of Wisconsin's forests. The process of
settlement and building which the Civil War had inter-
rupted was renewed and now, at last, some of the older
residents and some newcomers as well began to see new
opportunities in the state's more northerly counties.

Lumbering had begun on a small scale in Wisconsin in
the nineteenth century, and in the latter half of the century it became the biggest business of the region. The
seemingly unlimited number of growing cities and towns
required vast quantities of lumber, and Wisconsin's rich
pineries proved, for the time at least, to be equal to the
demand. Lumbermen continued to work half a dozen major districts in the state—the areas around Green Bay and
the Wolf, Wisconsin, Black, Chippewa, and St. Croix rivers. The lumbermen's frontier penetrated the area from

these rivers after a series of Indian treaties, beginning in 1836, opened the white pine timberlands to exploitation. Highly skilled raftsmen guided some of the logs down the rivers; other log rafts were slowly pulled across the Great Lakes by lake steamers which had been transformed into lumber barges.

The coming of the railroads brought a number of changes to lumbering. Railroad lines were built to more remote stands of timber and lumbering was no longer restricted to the river paths. The railroads also modified the marketing of lumber. The roads spanned the entire country and made it possible to sell Wisconsin pine in all

Rafting lumber down the Wisconsin River
H. H. Bennett Studios—SHSW Colls.

parts of the nation. In the course of a single year an Eau Claire lumber company sent five thousand carloads of its product to twenty-three different states and territories. The railroads themselves also created a new demand for lumber which provided material for fuel, cars, depots, ties, and bridges. By 1890, despite the higher cost of rail transportation, more Wisconsin lumber left the state on railroads than on the rivers.

The amount of lumber taken from Wisconsin forests increased each year until 1892 when lumbermen cut an estimated four billion feet. That proved to be the peak year for the industry. Although in 1900 Wisconsin still led all states in production of white pine lumber, from then on decline set in. The supply of timber proved, after all, to be limited, and the lumber barons turned increasingly to the untapped forest reserves of the South and Pacific Northwest to carry on their business. Extending the in-

The railroads greatly expanded the market for Wisconsin lumber
SHSW Colls.

Interior of a large sawmill, Chippewa Falls
SHSW Colls.

dustry to a national scale brought some disadvantages as
well as advantages. The lumbermen became subject to the
price demands of the railroads, and they found themselves
more at the mercy of national price fluctuations. When
hard times hit, as in 1873, lumbering suffered severely.
There were always a multitude of risks in the business.
Obstructions in the rivers caused log jams. Thieving trespassers cut much valuable timber from lands owned by
the lumber companies. Fires often roared through thousands of acres of wooded land and sometimes destroyed
lumber camps, mills, and cities as well. In 1871 Peshtigo
was destroyed by such a forest fire.

Unlike earlier and simpler operations, the large-scale lumbering of the later nineteenth century required a considerable investment of money. Lumbering also played its part in the era of the large corporation in American industry. By 1896, 68 corporations owned 168 of Wisconsin's lumber companies. In 1870 Frederick Weyerhaeuser

A Wisconsin lumber yard
SHSW Colls.

of Rockford, Illinois, and some of his Mississippi River associates organized the Mississippi River Logging Company, which was capitalized at $1,000,000. The company purchased valuable timberlands, fixed prices, and fought the Chippewa River lumbermen who regarded its intrusion as a threat to their older, loosely organized business. In 1880 the opposing groups came to terms. Weyerhaeuser then went on to demonstrate how big an operation lumbering could become. In 1881 he acquired a huge sawmill at Chippewa Falls for $1,275,000, and the following year he bought more than 100,000 acres of timberland for $1,841,756. Weyerhaeuser brought to lumbering the same kind of big business tactics, with its increased consolidation of power as well as improved efficiency, that John D. Rockefeller, Henry Villard, Philip Armour, and others used in different areas of the nation's business.

As the various lumber regions were stripped of their trees, the people in the nearby areas turned to other work. Instead of limiting themselves to the more rudimentary work of sawmilling and the processing of crude lumber, they began to produce finished wood products. Fond du Lac factories produced doors, sashes, blinds, furniture, wagons, caskets, and farm implements. By 1870 the city boasted five such wood manufacturing enterprises with a total valuation of $483,800. Some entrepreneurs, like German-born C. J. L. Meyer, in addition to lumbering and the manufacture of wood products, branched out in a number of industrial fields including railroading, and even iron mining. Oshkosh businessmen turned to flour milling and meatpacking as well as the manufacture of wooden products, especially matches. Neenah and Menasha became nationally known for their wooden pails, tubs, barrels, spokes, and hubs which they produced in huge quantities.

Closely related to the lumber industry was the production of paper, which also was in unprecedented demand in the years after the Civil War. Paper was needed for business records and private correspondence and most of all to feed the insatiable appetites of the rotary presses of the thousands of city newspapers. Wisconsin paper making had its modest beginnings in Milwaukee before the Civil War, when cotton rags were the main ingredient. In the early 1870's Americans began manufacturing paper from wood pulp and Wisconsin quickly assumed an important role in the industry. Paper mills mushroomed in the Fox River region and later in the upper Wisconsin valley where a combination of wood supply and water power provided the necessary resources. The industry made use of the poplar and spruce trees previously neglected by the lumbermen. Large producers of wood pulp and pulp paper operated plants at Appleton, Nekoosa, Port Edwards, Wausau, Rhinelander, Merrill, and Tomahawk. By 1905 Wisconsin ranked fifth among the states in paper production; 6,000 workers found employment in the state's 52 paper factories.

Bigness also characterized the operations of the paper manufacturers. In 1891 De Pere had the largest paper mill in the West. It specialized in a fine grade product with the company producing 150 tons a day in 14 different mills. Some of Wisconsin's paper manufacturers combined with their competitors in order to control the output and prices. Twenty-five concerns, most of them in Wisconsin, entered such an arrangement in 1902 only to be sued two years later by the Federal government under the Sherman Anti-Trust Act. In 1906 the government dissolved the holding corporation by a Supreme Court injunction. Concentration of power in the business of paper making in Wisconsin led to government intervention, just as in other industries and other states.

In some sections of Wisconsin farmers began to settle on land that had earlier been considered good only for timber. Railroads with lands to sell, private land promoters and some lumber companies popularized the idea of settling the cutover lands of northern Wisconsin. In 1895 a new state Board of Immigration concentrated on attracting immigrants and farmers to these lands. By 1897 50,000 copies of William A. Henry's *Northern Wisconsin: A Handbook for the Homeseeker* informed prospective settlers of the physiography, climate, soil, land prices, growing conditions, and economic possibilities of the cutover lands. A large proportion of those who started Wisconsin farms around the turn of the century dug their plows into soil which had been forest land a few years earlier. Yet despite the movement northward, millions of acres remained to be settled at a later time.

The steady expansion of railroads northward made possible this cutover settlement in Wisconsin. A building boom in railroads lasting from 1870 to 1890 brought a network of roads into the northern half of the state. By 1877 the Wisconsin Central had completed its line from Menasha to Ashland, the first of several connections between Lake Superior and the central part of Wisconsin. In less than a decade the Northern Pacific Railroad connected the Wisconsin towns of Ashland and Superior with Duluth, Minnesota and the West. With the railroad came new towns and new villages, the Wisconsin Central claiming credit for creating a whole series of settlements between 1870 and 1880, including Junction City, Marshfield, Dorchester, and Chippewa.

Railroading was another giant business that appeared to thrive on combination and consolidation. Besides new lines started at this time, older lines like the Chicago and North Western, and the Milwaukee and St. Paul roads con-

An early engine being transported over land

SHSW Colls

tinued to expand and to absorb shorter, branch lines as well. Alexander Mitchell was the business organizer behind the movement for the consolidation of Wisconsin railroads. By 1869 he controlled all the east-west railroads in Wisconsin and before his death in 1887 his company, reorganized in 1874 as the Chicago, Milwaukee and St. Paul, owned 5,660 miles of road in Wisconsin and other states. The other giant railroad operating in the area, the Chicago and North Western, was primarily a north-south series of roads. Both great lines connected Wisconsin with the booming prairie settlements to the south, the great plains area to the west, and beyond that to the rapidly settling Pacific coast region. Bigness in railroading, too, was the order of the day and the managers of the various huge concerns often found it possible to reach agreements on business matters. In 1869, for example, Alexander Mitchell was president of the North Western as well as of

Early passenger train

Train wrecks were common
SHSW Colls.

his own Milwaukee road. During much of that year Mitchell virtually controlled all the state's important railroads.

Such concentration of power brought new demands for control. Farmers, lumbermen, and settlers grumbled and complained once more about the unfair railroad practices and high rates. The complaints, aggravated by the hard times following the Panic of 1873, bore fruit in the Potter Law of the same year. It was the nation's first example of so-called Granger legislation, designed to check the power of the railroads by state action. The law, actually a concession to anti-railroad sentiment rather than to the Wisconsin Grange, was too extreme to be effective. It classified the roads and fixed maximum rates considerably below those currently in force. Two years later the Wisconsin legislature replaced the Potter Law with the more restrained Vance Act. But the Potter Law led to some important decisions for Wisconsin's future.

Alexander Mitchell and Albert Keep, the two biggest railroad magnates in the state, challenged the law in the courts. They contended that such an enactment was unconstitutional and announced that they would refuse to obey it. The State Supreme Court, under Chief Justice Edward G. Ryan, thought otherwise. In a famous book-length decision Ryan asserted the right of the state to check the power of private interests and laid the basis for future government intervention in business affairs. He pointed out that the new corporations, if "outside of public control, are dangerous to public and private right, and are practically above many public restraints of the common law, and all ordinary remedies of the common law for private wrongs." Ryan did not claim to oppose corporations as such, but said that they were subject to legislative control. The law was clearly constitutional, concluded Ryan, and it must be obeyed. Ryan's persuasive decision was widely discussed in legal circles and the opinions he put forth were later repeated many times in Wisconsin and in other states as well. Besides the principle of legislative control over corporations, one other feature of the Potter Law remained after the legislature had repealed the law itself. It had created a board of railroad commissioners to supervise the railroads; the Vance Act incorporated the same idea but provided for a single commissioner instead of a board.

Although Wisconsin's early Granger law furnished a precedent for other states, Wisconsin farmers gave only half-hearted support to the programs of agricultural protest that swept over so much of the Midwest in the 1870's and again in the 1890's. The farmers in the state had the same problems and complaints as their neighbors, but instead of joining a crusade against the moneyed interests of the East, many of them turned their efforts to new and profitable agricultural ventures. The last quarter of the nineteenth century was a time of considerable experimentation which led to an outstanding success in dairying. By 1900 the trend away from wheat farming, which had already begun during the boom days of the Civil War, had been completed.

The change was gradual and almost imperceptible. For years wheat seemed to be the most successful crop for Wisconsin farmers to raise. The new agricultural machinery made large yields possible, and wheat was easy to transport. However, farmers who planted wheat year after year eventually learned that it left the soil badly depleted. The per-acre yield declined. A pernicious chinch bug attacked the wheat and further cut into the farmers' profits. Then, too, the price of wheat declined as new agricultural areas in Asia and Europe began to compete with the American crop on the world market. Some farmers stubbornly refused to change, and sought new lands rather than new crops. As the soil in southern Wisconsin became exhausted, some of the wheat farmers took up lands to the north. Others left the state and opened farms in the new West of Kansas, Nebraska, and the Dakotas. The change-over was completed by 1870 when wheat was no longer king in the Badger State. In the decades between 1871 and 1891 the acreage of wheat planted in the state dropped from 3,572,000 to 1,889,000, or nearly 50 per cent. But Wisconsin was still attracting people. Farmers heading west often sold their holdings to others coming in, not infrequently to newly-arrived immigrants from Scandinavia, Poland, Bohemia, and other parts of Europe.

In the decade from 1870 to 1880 diversification characterized much of the production of Wisconsin farms. Along with the older staple, wheat, farmers raised corn, oats, hay crops, and livestock. For many, sheep raising seemed to be the next best thing to wheat farming. When

Slav immigrants
SHSW Colls.

woolen prices fell sheep growers switched to mutton breeds, and many raised horses, cows, and swine as well as sheep. Hogs thrived in sections where corn was raised as feed, and on many a Wisconsin farm they played the important role of "mortgage-lifters." Even when dairying finally became supreme, the farmers often combined it with raising hogs.

Wisconsin's rise to its position as a leading dairy state did not come about accidentally. After a few individuals had experimented successfully, a group of determined promoters persuaded Wisconsin farmers to become dairymen. The pioneers were mostly New Yorkers who had brought knowledge, skill, and experience with them from their native state where a highly successful dairy industry was already flourishing. The rich Wisconsin soil was well adapted to the raising of feeds and grasses and the industry developed at the very time when an expanding market encouraged its success. Milk as well as numerous manufactured dairy products were readily sold to the multitudes of Americans who lived in cities, far removed from farms and dairy cows.

Wisconsin dairy farmers first developed the cheese-making phase of the industry. In 1872, when only about forty-five or fifty cheese factories were in operation, a group of determined dairy promoters founded the Wisconsin Dairymen's Association, and their first victory was to prove to Wisconsin farmers that their product could compete successfully with New York cheese. The association arranged to ship cheese to the East by refrigerator cars. It held institutes, promoted scientific improvements in dairying, constantly advertised the product of the state, promoted the idea of a Dairy School, and lobbied for laws which protected its economic interests. William Dempster Hoard, an enthusiastic founder of the Association, led the crusade with numerous writings, speeches, and the publication of several newspapers. Hoard tried to convince farmers of the worth of a "single purpose milk cow," increased application of scientific knowledge to farming, and the value of silos to store cattle feed. The exhibition of Wisconsin cheese at the Philadelphia Centennial Exhibition in 1876 did more than any other single operation to put the Badger cheese makers into active competition with the New York interests. Soon production boomed and cheese left the Badger State for eastern city sales places as well as Liverpool, and other foreign ports. In 1890 more than 1,000 Wisconsin cheese factories produced 53,708,595 pounds of cheese with a market value of more than $4,000,000.

Dairying became a highly specialized industry and put farming on a more regulated basis. The farmers could no longer work solely on hours of their own preference but now had to adjust to the schedule most beneficial to milk production. And dairying, like other large industries, required capital. In the mid-1870's it cost approximately $800 to set up a cheese factory which could process the milk output of 400 cows. The entire production center of farm and factory might cost as much as $20,000. Butter making quickly followed cheese making, and each activity had its separate interests. At the turn of the century Dane, Walworth, Jefferson, and Rock were leading butter counties and Green County led in cheese production. Some cheese factories specialized in Swiss, while others produced limburger, brick, or other types of cheese. Eventually the cheese makers, butter makers, researchers, and dealers all had their own separate organizations. Even the Wisconsin Dairymen's Association proved to be too broad an organization in the highly specialized economy which was developing in the late nineteenth century. Yet adjusting to agricultural specialization enabled Wisconsin dairymen to succeed at a time when most other western farmers were in unusually bad straits. The number of cows in Wisconsin increased from around 64,000 in 1850 to 1,600,000 in 1890. Substituting Queen Cow for King Wheat saved the day for Wisconsin agriculture. It was the development of this important farm enterprise more than anything else that mitigated the influence of the agricultural protest movements in the state. The farmers were becoming successful businessmen themselves and they had relatively little to complain about.

One of the factors which made Wisconsin's transition to a dairy state less difficult was the presence and continual influx of European immigrants who flocked in large numbers to the state across the Great Lakes from eastern seaport centers. The Scandinavians, especially, were willing to undertake the routinized, skilled, and difficult tasks of caring for dairy cattle. When many Yankee-stock

---

THE IRISH IN WISCONSIN

The majority of Irish immigrants in northern Wisconsin eventually became farmers. By 1870 the town of Erin Prairie contained two hundred Irish families. Their situation was described by a correspondent of the St. Paul NORTHWESTERN CHRONICLE IN 1867:

The prosperity the Irish settlers on this prairie—and there are none others—have attained to within a few years, is wonderful, indeed, and refutes so thoroughly the ignorant and too frequently malicious slanderers—who taking some barroom loafer as a model, judge the Irish people from this low standard—that I have felt proud and happy to listen to many a settler's story of early trials and ultimate success.

Twelve years ago the first Irish settlers came into Erin Prairie with little or no capital, but brave hearts and strong arms; now the Irish have not alone possessed themselves of every acre of this fine prairie for six miles square, but they have spread out into the townships of Emerald, on the east, Hamond [sic] on the south, Warren, southwest, Richmond, west, and Star Prairie, north. In most instances the Irish who moved from Erin Prairie into those other townships bought improved farms, for which they paid from twenty to thirty dollars an acre; they did not go in quest of better land than they had where they first settled, for it would be impossible to find such; but, in order to have room to farm on a larger scale and they got ready purchasers in their neighbors, who remained, and were also anxious to enlarge their farms.—SISTER M. JUSTILLE McDONALD, F.S.P.A., "The Irish of the North Country," in the *Wisconsin Magazine of History*, 40:130–131 (Winter, 1956–1957).

American settlers left their Wisconsin farms for lands farther west rather than be "tied to a cow," newer arrivals from Norway, Denmark, Holland, Germany, Switzerland, and Bohemia acquired their farms and provided the skills and energy necessary to carry on a profitable dairy farm and manufacturing industry.

Some of the immigrant groups contributed other skills as well. Many of the Polish immigrants who came after 1870 staked out farms in Portage County only after they had first lived for a while in some of the larger American cities. Many of the Irish immigrants migrated to the northernmost counties where they found work as loggers, factory workers, and railroad hands, sometimes combining such occupations with farming until they could afford to purchase enough land to work it full time. Daughters of some of the German and Scandinavian immigrants became domestic servants, thus improving their English and acquiring a better understanding of American ways while providing a kind of service that was always scarce and much in demand in early Wisconsin.

The immigrants also brought new members for the Catholic, Lutheran, and Reformed faiths. With quaint Old World customs and clothing, and foreign words and phrases that sometimes became a part of the local vocabulary, they added richness and color to the Wisconsin scene. And they came in increasingly large numbers. In 1850 the foreign born population of Wisconsin was 110,-477; by 1890 it was nearly five times that number. That year's census indicated a native born population of 1,167,-681 and a foreign born one of 519,199. Of that number, 259,819 were from Germany, 99,838 from the Scandinavian countries, 99,888 from the British dominions, and the rest from Ireland, Scotland, Wales, Poland, Bohemia, Russia, Hungary, France, Italy, Austria, Holland, Belgium, Luxembourg, and Switzerland.

At the same time that immigrants were coming to Wisconsin in unprecedented numbers, more of the people of the state exchanged life on a farm for life in the city. In Wisconsin, as in the nation at large, cities became more important in American life after the Civil War. Each year the urban population of the state increased until in the decade from 1880 to 1890 the proportionate increase was greater for the urban than for the rural population, though it was not until the 1920's that more than half of Wisconsin's citizens lived in urban areas. The trend was caused by the movement of people from farms into the cities, and also by the arrival in cities of immigrants from the Old World. By 1905 Milwaukee led by far with a teeming population of 312,000, and Superior was second in size with 36,551. Eighty-six Wisconsin cities contained more than two thousand people each, and eighteen of them contained more than a third of the state's population. But the urban population surge was only one factor. Cities also grew increasingly important and vital to the rest of the nation because of their contributions as centers of industry, commerce, and culture. In these areas, too, Milwaukee was far in the lead.

Increased specialization characterized much of Milwaukee's growth and development in the later years of the nineteenth century. A Chamber of Commerce proudly advertised the city's desirability as a place to live and do business. A Medical Association contributed to the professionalization of medical service, and led a number of crusades for more and improved hospitals. It was not until 1870 that Milwaukee citizens had regular police protection and a semi-professional fire department replaced the earlier, completely volunteer force. A board of public works exercised general control over the city's streets, bridges, sidewalks and public buildings. The city government provided relief for the needy and in the fall of

1873 Milwaukee residents began obtaining water from a municipally-owned water works. Thus many services which had earlier been provided by individuals or private interests, as well as some which had not been provided at all, were supplied by the city itself. As Milwaukee grew in size, the need for an even greater number of professional and specialized services became apparent to many of its residents.

Milwaukee continued to be important as a trade center, but each year the city's various industrial plants attracted more attention, talent, and capital. Even though Chicago became the commercial metropolis that Milwaukee had hoped to become, the excellent location of the Wisconsin city ensured its rise as an industrial center. By 1873 as many as ten different railroad lines served the merchants, manufacturers, and citizens of the Cream City. A steamer line ran from Milwaukee to Ludington, Michigan, where it made connections with railroad lines traveling to the East Coast cities. Some of the heavy, bulky products from Milwaukee went via lake steamers directly to the East. With Milwaukee's continued industrial growth, transportation companies shifted their interest from the carrying of farm produce to transporting manufactured items. Instead of wheat and other farm products, the railroads and lake steamers began to carry more leather goods, heavy farm machinery, beer, and meat products from Milwaukee; and city wholesalers in turn imported numerous items from the East.

Milwaukee industries supplied local residents and people in the Wisconsin hinterland with clothing, flour, beer, leather goods, meat, and farm machinery. But some of these industries had outgrown the local demand, and more and more Milwaukee-made products found their way to distant markets. Milwaukee-tanned leather supplied the raw material for Boston's shoe factories, engines from Edward P. Allis and Company provided power for Pittsburgh's steel factories, and Harnischfeger cranes lifted countless steel beams in the expanding cities throughout America. The two leading Milwaukee breweries each produced more than a million barrels of beer between 1873 and 1893, and the beverage quenched the thirst of people all over the world. Admiral Peary found a Pabst bottle as he approached the North Pole, and the Schlitz company dispatched 3,600 bottles of its product to the tropics for Admiral Dewey's men after the capture of Manila.

A number of new scientific findings contributed to the success of some of Milwaukee's huge industries. Refrigerated railroad cars enabled the meatpackers to ship their goods long distances without spoilage. An important innovation in the tanning industry, the substitution of the chemical tannin for tanbark, made it unnecessary to locate the tanneries in forested areas and encouraged the concentration of the leather industry in the city itself. The breweries hired professional chemists to improve their beer and used refrigerator plants, underground vats, underground pipe lines from the cellars to the bottling works, and electric lights for night work. After making a study of the effect of light on beer the Schlitz company adopted the famous brown bottles. These and other advances were made possible because of the large-scale nature of Milwaukee industry. By 1900 Pfister and Vogel, a tanning company, owned five tanneries with marketing branches in Boston and New York as well as in four cities in Great Britain, and on the continent of Europe. By 1885 the Bay View Iron Works was owned by the North Chicago Rolling Mill Company which owned mills in the Midwest worth $5,000,000. Later combinations brought the Milwaukee plants into the giant United States Steel Corporation in 1901.

Some of Milwaukee's largest industrial concerns grew out of earlier, small-scale business ventures of enterprising economic pioneers like Edward P. Allis, who emigrated to Milwaukee from New York in 1846 when he was only twenty-two. A graduate of Union College, he had hoped to study law but the business opportunities of Wisconsin diverted him from his youthful professional ambitions. With a partner from New York, Allis opened a leather store which proved so profitable that within a few years the partners, along with some others, started a tannery at Two Rivers. In 1856 Allis temporarily withdrew from active business, but in 1861 he purchased the Reliance Iron Works which became Edward P. Allis and Company, and was the nucleus for his most important business venture.

The company specialized in equipment for flour mills and did a booming business supplying the machinery for Wisconsin's many mills and also the mills of Minnesota and other parts of the northwest. In 1867 the Milwaukee *Sentinel* reported that the Allis Company employed seventy-five workers and had annual receipts of about $50,000. In the 1870's Allis added the manufacture of water pipe to his activities and won lucrative contracts for pipe and steam driven pumps from both Milwaukee and Chicago. Allis was hard hit by the depression of the 70's and forced into bankruptcy in 1876. For several years he diverted much of his energy into political channels, supporting the cause of greenback money, so popular with Western debtor groups. Allis ran unsuccessfully for the office of governor on the Greenback ticket in 1877 and 1881.

During his political career Allis had a group of unusually competent subordinates to carry on his business. Among them was the gifted engineer-inventor Edwin Reynolds, who had helped develop the fine Corliss heavy duty steam engine. The Allis Company soon brought out an improved Reynolds-Corliss engine used in mines, sawmills, power plants, and urban water works. Despite some labor troubles in the 1880's, the Allis Company continued to grow. In 1890 it was the largest manufacturing concern in Milwaukee with nearly 1,500 employees and a national reputation for excellent products. After Allis's death in 1889 the company was reorganized and in 1901 it merged with three other similar companies located in Chicago and Scranton, Pennsylvania. As Allis-Chalmers the company's annual business exceeded $10,000,000 and was Wisconsin's largest manufacturer of heavy machinery, and among the leaders of the entire nation in this field, with branch offices in foreign as well as American cities.

Allis started his business at a time when agriculture was supreme and his high quality machinery for flour mills served the industry which was so closely tied in with wheat farming. When cities required pipe and steam pumps for their water works, Allis supplied them and later the production of heavy duty steam engines echoed another trend in an industrializing America. When nearly all the farms became industrialized, Allis-Chalmers led in the production of tractors and other farm machinery. And in the age of electricity the Milwaukee firm turned to the manufacture of fine quality electrical equipment. The contribution of Edward P. Allis and his successors illustrates some of the changes which took place in Wisconsin and emphasizes the fundamental role of heavy industry even in a region where agriculture remains significant.

While Milwaukee was developing into a leading industrial city, it grew in size and took on more of a cosmopolitan tone. Its population boomed from 71,440 to 373,-857 in the years from 1870 to 1910, many of the people being immigrants from other lands. A third of its people were natives of Germany who gave their adopted city a German appearance. Milwaukee had Germanic singing societies, athletic associations, German language newspapers and beer gardens. But the German element was only one of the city's immigrant groups, and towards the end of the century other Europeans came in large numbers. The new arrivals—Czechs, Slovaks, Italians, Russian Jews, and Poles—proved to be more clannish than the Germans and less easily assimilated into the main stream of American life. Like the Germans, they had their own associations, church groups, and press, but they seemed to be more determined to hold on to their own customs. By the time the newer immigrant groups began to be noticed, some of the older German families were becoming more American than German. The social standing of such men as Frederick Pabst, Christian Wahl, Joseph Schlitz, and other German-Americans was based on a

Militia guarding the Allis plant

SHSW Colls.

MAY 5, 1886.

combination of achievement and wealth. Eventually the German background of many such pioneer families seemed less important than their wealth, or their various contributions to the life of the city.

Milwaukee grew more rapidly than most American cities and probably had a higher percentage of the newer immigrants, but this was only a matter of degree. Other cities throughout the nation were also attracting myriads of discontented Europeans who for one reason or another came to believe that they could improve their economic position in America. In other ways, too, Milwaukee experienced changes that were characteristic of the growing industrial centers of late nineteenth century America. One of these developments was the appearance of an effective labor movement. Unionism had gone beyond the earlier, fraternal-type organization of highly skilled workers, and by the 1880's there were strong unions of iron and steel workers and other factory laborers. The unions sometimes entered local politics and in 1886 widespread strikes and participation in the nationwide eight-hour-day movement brought labor violence to Milwaukee. Paul Grottkau, labor editor, Socialist, and leader of the Central Labor Union, led one faction demanding the eight-hour day. Energetic and crusading Robert Schilling of the Knights of Labor led another. In a short time Schilling was able to organize fifty lodges of the Knights totaling a membership of sixteen thousand. It was Schilling and his followers who spearheaded the eight-hour-day movement in May, 1886. After several days of strikes and near violence, Governor Jeremiah Rusk felt it necessary to call out the state militia to maintain order in the city. Among the militia sent into Milwaukee was a Polish Kosciuszco Guard and its presence angered some of the Polish strikers. The Guard, under orders to shoot to kill if necessary, fired into strikers at the Bay View Iron Works, killing eight and injuring a number of others. Governor Rusk justified his order saying, "I seen my duty and I done it." The governor gained national fame for his ungrammatical remark, the eight-hour-day movement collapsed in defeat, and Milwaukee labor unions turned once again to politics to make known their grievances.

During the period of rapid growth and industrialization with its accompanying labor unrest, Milwaukee was also developing as a cultural center. In 1880 the Milwaukee Public Library boasted fifteen thousand volumes, and in 1898 the expanding collection enjoyed a new building of its own. Even though one theatrical agent characterized Milwaukee as "the poorest theatrical city in the United States," many of its residents turned out to see such outstanding actors as Edwin Booth and Sarah Bernhardt. Probably a larger number of them enjoyed diversions offered by numerous traveling minstrel shows and a Dime Museum with "The Frog Child" and "Barnum's Fiji Cannibals" as featured attractions. German drama also flourished under the sponsorship of the city's German theatre. Stock companies with such popular offerings as *Humpty Dumpty Abroad* had no trouble filling the house. Large numbers also attended musical performances, including occasional concerts like the 1884 appearance of Theodore Thomas conducting the magnificent Chicago Symphony Orchestra.

Along with the interest in the theatre and musical performances went an improvement in Milwaukee's educational opportunities. Besides numerous private schools and academies, the city's youth also had access to a growing public school system. In 1870 Milwaukee spent $93,-000 for its school system, which by 1910 included four high schools. However, not everybody shared these advantages. Only about half the school-age residents were attending schools in 1910.

Yet despite the large number of Milwaukee children not attending schools, the city's educational opportunities were better than those in many other places in Wisconsin. Although most people eventually and sometimes grudgingly accepted the idea of public support for elementary education, they had to be convinced all over again when the issue of tax-supported high schools was proposed. There were private academies available for those who could afford to attend them and some of their supporters even argued that public high schools were unconstitutional. By 1873 about thirty Wisconsin cities provided some tax-supported schooling beyond the eighth grade, but it was only after 1874 that the movement gained momentum. That was the year Michigan's supreme court handed down the Kalamazoo decision which established the legality of using public funds to support high schools. The following year a Wisconsin law provided for the establishment of public high schools and by 1880 there were more than a hundred secondary school districts throughout the state.

Even the educators did not agree about the purpose of the new schools. Some argued for a classical education for all, insisting that such subjects as Greek and Latin were essential for any students planning to enter the university, and good discipline for those who were not. Others believed that mental training was less important than education for good citizenship, and there were advocates of industrial and agricultural training as well. In practice there was much diversity and it was not until 1880 that the state exercised any direct supervision over its high schools. Towards the end of the century Wisconsin became a leader in the field of vocational education and later in the education of the physically and mentally handicapped.

While the university was the highest rung in the state's

educational ladder, many preferred to attend the various other Wisconsin colleges. A number of state normal schools trained teachers of elementary and secondary subjects. Wisconsin's first normal school opened at Platteville in 1866 and two years later another was established at Whitewater. Before the turn of the century others were located in Oshkosh, River Falls, Milwaukee, La Crosse and Eau Claire. By 1916 Stevens Point and Superior also had state normal schools. At first these teacher training institutions accepted students who had not completed high school and offered them a variety of courses of different lengths designed to prepare teachers for various types of elementary and secondary schools. After 1899 a number of county normal schools also supplied Wisconsin's rural schools with teachers who had two years of training beyond high school.

Many of the public school instructors were trained in the state's private colleges rather than in the various normal schools. Most of the private institutions of higher learning were founded by religious groups who wanted to provide an education which would also indoctrinate students for a particular faith. The outstanding Catholic college was Marquette, founded in 1881, which became a university in 1907. A number of the sectarian colleges were founded before the Civil War: Beloit by Presbyterians and Congregationalists in 1846, Carroll by the Presbyterians the same year, Lawrence by the Methodists in 1847, and Ripon, changed from an academy to a college in 1863, was nominally non-sectarian but most of its presidents were from the Congregational ministry. Two women's colleges, Milwaukee and Downer, merged as Milwaukee-Downer College in 1891. Most of the early sectarian colleges later dropped their close connections with the churches that founded them. However, Carroll College is still Presbyterian, Milton College is Seventh Day Baptist, Northwestern College at Watertown is connected with the Lutheran Church, and Northland College at Ashland is Congregational. Thousands of young people have been trained for careers in teaching, the ministry, medicine, and business in Wisconsin's private colleges.

While Wisconsin's numerous educators were training citizens for life in a changing era, a number of Wisconsin inventors devised new objects and added improvements to others which helped direct the changes and hasten the pace of their adoption. As early as 1844 Jerome I. Case designed a successful combined thresher and wheat separator which he later manufactured at his Racine plant. In 1878 John Francis Appleby, after many discouraging years of trial and error, placed a practical twine binder on the market. The earlier wire binders had proved unsatisfactory for grain because small pieces of broken wire damaged the machinery and killed the cattle when they were swallowed along with the feed. The Appleby binder solved the problem and was quickly accepted by farmers who grew wheat and other grains.

Other Wisconsin inventors created an improved engine, a light, self-propelled vehicle, a cheese press, a type-making machine, an electric crane, soda water apparatus, and a wood carving machine. William Horlick of Racine invented malted milk. John Stevens of Neenah devised a modern roller-type flour mill and his admirers disputed those who claimed that the process of rolling flour began in Hungary. Wisconsin inventions made far reaching contributions to the era of industrialism and mechanized farming, but two stand out above all the rest: the Babcock milk tester and the typewriter.

In 1890 Stephen M. Babcock, a professor of dairy husbandry at the University of Wisconsin College of Agriculture, discovered that a small amount of sulfuric acid added to a measured amount of milk and whirled in a simple machine would bring the fat to the surface where it could easily be measured. Prior to the invention of Babcock's tester, it was virtually impossible to determine the exact amount of butterfat in milk without a chemical analysis. His invention made it impossible for farmers to dilute their milk and further encouraged the rise of an already important dairy industry in Wisconsin. It was only the most important of a series of contributions that university scientists made to Wisconsin's economic development. For his milk tester Professor Babcock received many honors, including a *grand prix d'honneur* at the

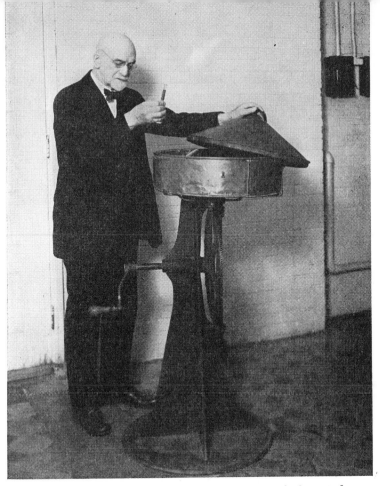

Babcock's butterfat tester revolutionized Wisconsin's dairy industry. *SHSW Colls.*

Paris exposition in 1900, but the inventor refused to patent his work and unselfishly shared his findings with dairymen throughout the world.

The Babcock tester was a very simple device, but the typewriter was about as complicated as a machine could be. The inventor, Christopher Latham Sholes of Milwaukee, finally succeeded where at least twenty others had failed. Sholes' first writing machine, demonstrated in 1867, looked like a combination piano and kitchen table.

The early models had many irritating defects, but an unusually imaginative promoter, James Densmore, kept prodding Sholes into making additional improvements. Densmore also assured the pessimistic and discouraged inventor that eventually the typewriter would be a commercial success. The Remington Company of New York began manufacturing typewriters in 1874 but the gadget was only a curiosity, and its price of $125 proved to be too high for most of its prospective buyers. But by 1888 the

---

THE TYPEWRITER

By September, 1869, Christopher Latham Sholes of Milwaukee had perfected his invention of a writing machine to the point where he was enthusiastic in describing the result to James Densmore, his friend and promoter:

Its simplicity cannot be equalled, it being more simple if possible than a piano, and so less liable to get out of order. A child may thump its keys with pleasure and do it no harm. It works, also, as easily as a piano is manipulated. I am inclined to think that in a day's writing the use of the pen would be found much more tiresome than the use of this machine. As to rapidity I am working this about as fast as ordinary writing, say twenty words a minute, but I, you know, am getting old and clumsy and not the person to readily take on new practices. It is susceptible, I have no doubt, of being worked at the rate of sixty words a minute, and some are sanguine enough to believe that a hundred may be worked. A few may reach the latter number, possibly, but I am content to average, on practice, at sixty, which being from twice to three times as fast as writing, is satisfactory.—Sholes to Densmore, September, 1869, quoted in RICHARD N. CURRENT, *The Typewriter and the Men Who Made It* (Urbana, Ill., 1954), 32.

Remington plant, operated by a group of enthusiastic promoters who had taken over the typewriter phase of the business two years before, turned out 1,500 typewriters a month. Both inventor Sholes and promoter Densmore realized profit from the invention, although Sholes received only $40,000 for his efforts. Besides providing employment for countless women, the typewriter quickly assumed its place as an absolute necessity in the era of big business of the late nineteenth century, as well as in the era of big government that followed it.

TERMS OF WISCONSIN'S GOVERNORS, 1878–1906

January, 1878–1882   William E. Smith (Republican)
January, 1882–1889   Jeremiah M. Rusk (Republican)
January, 1889–1891   William D. Hoard (Republican)
January, 1891–1895   George W. Peck (Democrat)
January, 1895–1897   William H. Upham (Republican)
January, 1897–1901   Edward Scofield (Republican)
January, 1901–1906   Robert M. La Follette (Republican)

—*Wisconsin Blue Book*, 1915 (Madison, 1915), 367.

In fact, in Wisconsin as in other states, there was little distinction made in theory or in practice between business and politics. Both political parties subscribed to the same basic program, but in Wisconsin, Republican politicians had little effective opposition; between 1856 and 1891 the state had only one Democratic governor. Philetus Sawyer of Oshkosh, the new Republican boss of Wisconsin, was a shrewd, homespun political leader who had acquired a fortune as a lumberman. After serving a decade in Congress, Sawyer joined other masters of wealth in the United

States Senate. In Washington he strongly supported many internal improvement measures, a high protective tariff, generous pensions for Civil War veterans, and equally generous federal subsidies for railroads. Sawyer's enemies called him the "curbstone statesman" of Oshkosh, but his apparent concern for his constituents and his friendship with many influential national and state political leaders enabled him to dole out patronage, choose candidates, and win elections. He personally chose John C. Spooner, a wealthy railroad attorney from Hudson, as his partner in the Senate, and Jeremiah Rusk, who served three terms, as governor. Sawyer was a good example of the kind of wealthy businessman who became a political boss; he and others like him replaced older-style political leaders like Boss Elisha W. Keyes, who had merely acted as intermediary spokesman for the business interests of the state.

As long as Republicanism seemed to bring lush and continued prosperity, few Wisconsinites objected to the party's obvious business connections. The Spanish-American War, with its short-lived popular crusade against European "barbarism" and its demonstration of America's military might, also strengthened the Republican cause. The brief conflict was a Republican war and it proved to be a popular one, requiring relatively few sacrifices. All four of Wisconsin's National Guard regiments were called to duty, but only two of them actually saw active service before the fighting ended.

The program which Wisconsin's Democrats supported was little different from that of the Republicans. The Democratic Party contained a number of factions but Boss William F. Vilas represented the pro-business, or "Bourbon," element. Vilas was a good friend of President Grover Cleveland, another conservative Democrat, and as Postmaster-General, Secretary of Interior, and as senator he lent his support to the railroad and industrial in-

1880	James A. Garfield (Republican)	144,400
	Winfield S. Hancock (Democrat)	114,649
	James B. Weaver (Greenback)	7,986
	J. B. Phelps (American)	91
	Neal Dow (Prohibition)	68

1884	James G. Blaine (Republican)	161,157
	Grover Cleveland (Democrat)	146,577
	John P. St. John (Prohibition)	7,656
	Benjamin F. Butler (Greenback)	4,598

1888	Benjamin Harrison (Republican)	176,555
	Grover Cleveland (Democrat)	155,232
	Clinton B. Fisk (Prohibition)	14,277
	A. J. Streeter (Union Labor)	8,552

1892	Grover Cleveland (Democrat)	177,335
	Benjamin Harrison (Republican)	170,846
	John Bidwell (Prohibition)	13,136
	James B. Weaver (Populist)	10,019

1896	William McKinley (Republican)	268,051
	William J. Bryan (Democrat)	165,389
	Joshua Levering (Prohibition)	7,507
	John M. Palmer (National Democrat)	4,584
	Charles H. Matchett (Soc. Labor)	1,314
	Charles E. Bentley (National)	346

1900	William McKinley (Republican)	265,866
	William J. Bryan (Democrat)	159,285
	John G. Wooley (Prohibition)	10,027
	Eugene V. Debs (Social Democrat)	7,048
	Joseph F. Malloney (Socialist Labor)	503

terests of the Middle West. As an ardent defender of the gold standard, he vigorously opposed those Democrats who wanted the party to undertake a crusade for inflation and to emphasize other demands of the farmers and the debtor classes. It was no surprise then that when Wisconsin voters elected a Democratic governor in 1890 the victorious candidate was George W. Peck, a humorist-editor and a solidly conservative Bourbon Democrat.

The Democratic victory of that year was more a symptom of the times than an indication of Republican weakness in Wisconsin. Some local Republicans charged that the upset resulted from the Bennett Law of 1889 which plugged loopholes in earlier school attendance legislation and required all schools to offer instruction in English rather than in a foreign language. The Democrats capitalized on the unpopularity of the measure among foreign groups and those who supported private schools. When the votes were counted Senator Spooner declared: "The defeat was inevitable. The school law did it—a silly, sentimental and damned useless abstraction, foisted upon us by a self-righteous demagogue." But Spooner was probably trying to divert attention from his own support of another highly unpopular measure, a tariff act. In fact a number of national issues helped to determine the Wisconsin election result. President Benjamin Harrison's billion-dollar Congress with its extravagant pork barrel spending, an ill-advised attempt to apply military force again to control southern elections, the tariff, and the arbitrary behavior of Speaker of the House Thomas B. Reed, all led to a reaction which was reflected in the state elections of 1890. In the same year the Democrats also won sweeping victories in Illinois, Michigan, Minnesota, and Nebraska. In 1892 Wisconsin's twelve electoral votes went to Cleveland but only 6,489 more residents of the state voted for him than for Harrison. In the congressional contest four Republicans won along with six Democrats. Two years earlier only one Republican had been elected to Congress.

Despite the combination of circumstances which enabled them to elect a governor, Wisconsin Democrats could not maintain power for long. They skillfully capitalized on Republican corruption when they instituted a series of lawsuits against former state treasurers for interest payments on state funds which were deposited in various banks. The treasurers had appropriated such interest payments for themselves and their political party and in the 1880's the amount was sometimes as high as $30,000 a year. The state won the suits which resulted from the Democratic exposé and in 1893 the Wisconsin supreme court upheld the judgments. The cases against the treasurers resulted in the return of approximately $373,000 before 1895 when a Republican-dominated legislature called a halt to the suits which were not yet settled.

Democratic political leaders, too, appeared willing to utilize questionable means to maintain power. Their flagrant attempts to reapportion the state into a series of cleverly gerrymandered districts twice met with defeat when the supreme court refused to lend it constitutional sanction. Such activity further aroused the suspicions of those who thought that Wisconsin's Democrats were too susceptible to corruption themselves and too deeply involved in their association with big business tycoons to become a reform party. Senator Vilas's loyalty to President Cleveland and his policies strengthened these suspicions. Wisconsin's other Democratic senator, John L. Mitchell, was the son of Alexander Mitchell and a representative of the big railroad interests. The economic crash of 1893 with its ensuing depression also tended to discredit the national Democratic administration. By 1894

Wisconsin's congressmen, legislators, and governor were again Republican. But within a few years the Republican Party itself found it necessary to adjust to a new set of circumstances. Out of that need for change emerged the Progressive movement, and it was Wisconsin that supplied its most famous leader.

Robert Marion La Follette, who became the foremost Progressive leader in America, was a graduate of the University of Wisconsin, a university which had also adapted itself to a world of change and specialization. In the latter quarter of the nineteenth century a combination of high quality leadership, idealism towards scholarship, and a program of service to the people of the state made the University an outstanding institution. The foundations which were laid during these years prepared the University to play a significant role in progressive reform and also in the scholarly activity of the entire country.

From 1874 to 1902 three unusually capable educators served as presidents of the University of Wisconsin. John Bascom, president from 1874 to 1887, came to Wisconsin after serving as president of Williams College. Bascom, who had many academic interests, was an active scholar whose textbooks in the fields of psychology, esthetics, rhetoric, and political economy were pioneer works. Bascom found it difficult to work with the Board of Regents, he had a drawn-out feud with Regent "Boss" Keyes, and eventually he resigned because of his lack of freedom. In some of his writings President Bascom attempted to reconcile science and religion, becoming a forerunner of the social gospel idea of promoting reform through applied Christianity. He feared too great a concentration of wealth in the hands of a few and advocated a graduated income tax, effective government action against monopolies, and legal measures to prevent gambling on the stock market. Among other controversial reforms he favored prohibition and woman suffrage. It was Bascom's hope that the University would help create the ideal Christian state in Wisconsin. His principal contribution to the University was his own personal example of excellent scholarship combined with a motivation of contagious idealism. Under his administration the University obtained new income from taxation, became truly co-educational and added several new buildings to its expanding campus. In a real sense President John Bascom was a founder of the Wisconsin idea in education which was to bear fruit at a later time.

Thomas C. Chamberlain became president when Bascom resigned and he held the post until 1892. A noted geologist, Chamberlain continued the emphasis on the development of Wisconsin's academic program which had been started by his predecessor. Under his leadership Wisconsin attracted to Madison some of Johns Hopkins' leading scholars, including, among others, economist Richard T. Ely, psychologist Joseph Jastrow, and historian C. H. Haskins. Ely became the head of a new school of Economics, Political Science, and History which, during its brief lifetime, made Wisconsin a leader of research and teaching in these areas. President Chamberlain also reorganized the University into separate, specialized divisions which included the Colleges of Letters and Science, Mechanics and Engineering, Agriculture, and Law. He too emphasized the need to train unselfish leaders as well as qualified specialists. It was under his administration that Frederick Jackson Turner, a native of Wisconsin and a graduate of the University, joined the history faculty. Turner became famous for his much-discussed theory which gave great significance to the frontier in American history.

Historian Charles Kendall Adams became president of

Frederick Jackson Turner
SHSW Colls.

TURNER'S FRONTIER THESIS

At the Chicago meeting of the American Historical Association in 1893, Wisconsin's young historian, Frederick Jackson Turner, first read his paper on "The Significance of the Frontier in American History." It has inspired more discussion and controversy than any other scholarly writing in the field of American history. The following excerpt contains the heart of Turner's thesis:

Up to our own day American history has been in a large degree the history of the colonization of the Great West. The existence of an area of free land, its continuous recession, and the advance of American settlement westward, explain American development. Behind institutions, behind constitutional forms and modifications, lie the vital forces that call these organs into life, and shape them to meet changing conditions. Now, the peculiarity of American institutions is the fact that they have been compelled to adapt themselves to the changes of an expanding people—to the changes involved in crossing a continent, in winning a wilderness, and in developing at each area of this progress out of the primitive economic and political conditions of the frontier into the complexity of city life. Said Calhoun in 1817, "We are great, and rapidly—I was about to say fearfully —growing!" So saying he touched the distinguishing feature of American life. . . . This perennial rebirth, this fluidity of American life, this expansion westward with its new opportunities, its continuous touch with the simplicity of primitive society, furnish the forces dominating American character. . . .

Since the days when the fleet of Columbus sailed into the waters of the New World, America has been another name for opportunity, and the people of the United States have taken their tone from the incessant expansion which has not only been open but has even been forced upon them. He would be a rash prophet who should assert that the expansive character of American life has now entirely ceased. Movement has been its dominant fact, and unless this training has no effect upon a people, the American intellect will continually demand a wider field for its exercise.—FREDERICK JACKSON TURNER in State Historical Society of Wisconsin, *Proceedings*, 1894, quoted in the *Wisconsin Magazine of History*, 40:90 (Winter, 1956–1957).

the University in 1892 when Chamberlain left to resume his scholarly work as head of the University of Chicago's Department of Geology. Adams's administration added little new, but under him the institution grew in size and continued to enjoy a nationwide reputation for excellent scholarship. By 1902, when Adams resigned because of poor health, the student population of the University exceeded two thousand.

It was during Adams's presidency that the University underwent an important test and challenge to the academic freedom of its teachers. In 1892 Oliver E. Wells, state superintendent of public instruction and *ex officio* member of the Board of Regents, accused Professor Richard T. Ely of favoring strikes and boycotts. The charge was untrue and the board refused to censure Ely. Instead it issued a statement which strongly asserted the right of teachers to "be absolutely free to follow the indications of truth wherever they may lead" in any line of academic investigation. "Whatever may be the limitations which trammel inquiry elsewhere," said the regents, "we believe the great University of Wisconsin should ever encourage that continual and fearless sifting and winnowing by which alone the truth can be found." The forthright declaration brought new acclaim to the University which was rapidly becoming a leader in American higher education.

The University served the people of the state in many ways. The department of agriculture and later the College of Agriculture published bulletins containing information useful to the farmers, carried on experiments, and held short courses and farmers' institutes. Leading authorities at work on the Madison campus trained engineers, lawyers, and teachers. A series of special lectures and correspondence courses carried learning from Bascom Hill to the far corners of the state. Summer courses, first for teachers and later for others as well, enabled some to take college work who were unable to study during the school year. The University helped bring prosperity to Wiscon-

Babcock with part of the University herd
SHSW Colls.
A Wisconsin barn raising, about 1890

sin in this time of change. In 1893 a pioneer member of the Board of Regents pointed out: "There is not a county in Wisconsin which is not richer because of the university. The cheese of Sheboygan, the butter of Rock, the tobacco of Dane, the sheep of Walworth, the horses and cattle of Racine and Kenosha, and the potatoes of Waupaca are all better because of our university, while the existence of those men who dig in the sunless mines of Gogebic has been made comparatively comfortable and safe through the discoveries of science."

Yet the contribution of the University of Wisconsin was greater than any material improvement it may have furthered. True, in a time of rapid change it helped citizens of the state to adapt themselves intelligently to a different way of life based on industrialization and specialization. But in the years ahead Wisconsin offered a new idea to democratic government in the form of the Progressive movement. And the combination of patriotic idealism, opposition to corruption, and the use of scholarly experts to provide a sound basis for an improved society owed much to the institution on the shores of Lake Mendota.

SUGGESTED ADDITIONAL READING

Anderson, Theodore A. *A Century of Banking in Wisconsin* (Madison, 1954), 54–97.

Blegen, Theodore C. "The Competition of the Northwestern States for Immigrants," in the *Wisconsin Magazine of History*, 3:3–29 (September, 1919).

Burnette, O. Lawrence, Jr., comp. *Wisconsin Witness to Frederick Jackson Turner: A Collection of Essays on the Historian and the Thesis* (Madison, 1961).

Campbell, Henry C. *Wisconsin in Three Centuries, 1634–1905* (4 vols., New York, 1906), Vol. IV.

Clark, James I. *Education in Wisconsin* (Madison, 1958).

————. *Edward P. Allis: Pioneer Industrialist* (Madison, 1958).

————. *Farm Machinery in Wisconsin* (Madison, 1956).

————. *Farming the Cutover: The Settlement of Northern Wisconsin* (Madison, 1956).

————. *Wisconsin Agriculture: The Rise of the Dairy Cow* (Madison, 1956).

————. *The Wisconsin Pineries: Logging on the Chippewa* (Madison, 1956).

————. *The Wisconsin Pulp and Paper Industry* (Madison, 1956).

Cochran, Thomas C. *The Pabst Brewing Company* (New York, 1948).

Current, Richard N. *Pine Logs and Politics: A Life of Philetus Sawyer, 1816–1900* (Madison, 1950).

————. *The Typewriter and the Men Who Made It* (Urbana, Illinois, 1954).

Curti, Merle and Carstensen, Vernon. *The University of Wisconsin: A History, 1848–1925* (2 vols., Madison, 1949), I, 246–739.

Fries, Robert F. *Empire in Pine: The Story of Lumbering in Wisconsin, 1830–1900* (Madison, 1951).

Gates, Paul W. "Weyerhaeuser and Chippewa Logging Industry," in O. Fritiof Ander, ed., *The John H. Hauberg Historical Essays* (Rock Island, Ill., 1954), 50–64.

————. *The Wisconsin Pine Lands of Cornell University: A Study in Land Policy and Absentee Ownership* (Ithaca, N. Y., 1943).

Glover, W. H. *Farm and College: The College of Agriculture of the University of Wisconsin, a History* (Madison, 1952).

Gregory, John G. "Foreign Immigration to Wisconsin," in the *Proceedings of the State Historical Society of Wisconsin, 1901*: 137–143.

Helgeson, Arlan. "Nineteenth Century Land Colonization in Northern Wisconsin," in the *Wisconsin Magazine of History*, 36: 115–121 (Winter, 1952–1953).

————. "The Wisconsin Treasury Cases," in the *Wisconsin Magazine of History*, 35:129–136 (Winter, 1951–1952).

Hunt, Robert S. *Law and Locomotives: The Impact of the Railroad on Wisconsin Law in the Nineteenth Century* (Madison, 1958).

Johnson, Peter Leo. *Crosier on the Frontier: A Life of John Martin Henni* (Madison, 1959).

Kellogg, Louise Phelps. "The Bennett Law in Wisconsin," in the *Wisconsin Magazine of History,* 2:3–25 (September, 1918).

Lampard, Eric E. *The Rise of the Dairy Industry in Wisconsin* (Madison, 1962).

Lawson, Publius V. "Paper-Making in Wisconsin," in State Historical Society of Wisconsin *Proceedings,* 1909: 273–280.

Martin, Xavier. "The Belgians of Northeast Wisconsin," in the *Wisconsin Historical Collections,* 13:375–396.

McDonald, Sister M. Justille. "The Irish of the North Country," in the *Wisconsin Magazine of History,* 40:126–132 (Winter, 1956–1957).

Merrill, Horace S. *Bourbon Democracy of the Upper Middle West, 1865–1898* (Baton Rouge, La., 1953).

————. *William Freeman Vilas: Doctrinaire Democrat* (Madison, 1954).

Raney, William Francis. *Wisconsin: A Story of Progress* (New York, 1940), 262–280.

Richardson, Helen L. D. "The Beloit College Agency," in the *Wisconsin Magazine of History,* 40:247–254 (Summer, 1957).

Sanford, Albert Hart. "Polish People of Portage County," in State Historical Society of Wisconsin *Proceedings,* 1907:259–288.

Schafer, Joseph. *A History of Agriculture in Wisconsin* (Madison, 1922).

Stephenson, Isaac. *Recollections of a Long Life, 1829–1915* (Chicago, 1915).

Still, Bayrd. *Milwaukee: The History of a City* (Madison, 1948), 257–430.

Thompson, John G. *The Rise and Decline of the Wheat Growing Industry in Wisconsin* (Madison, 1909).

Underwood, Harold G. "Wisconsin's Contribution to American Inventions," in State Historical Society of Wisconsin *Proceedings,* 1901:163–169.

CHAPTER 6

The Progressive Era in
Wisconsin
1900–1924

IN THE first quarter of the twentieth century new conditions led Wisconsin leaders to seek new answers to some
of the problems of a growing technological society. The
continued migration to the cities, the increased importance of industrialism, and the quickened pace of living
all brought bewilderment and confusion to people who
had been born, reared, and educated in a primarily
agricultural society.

From a purely economic standpoint, there was very
little basis for discontent. Wisconsin farmers continued
to receive good prices for their crops and dairy products,
and most of them owned the land they worked. The

products of Wisconsin's numerous industrial concerns also found a ready market throughout the nation and in other countries as well. By 1923 Wisconsin ranked tenth among the states in terms of the annual value of its industrial output, which then exceeded $1,700,000,000. But high prosperity and a growing economy did not produce contentment among many of the people of the state.

The new economic endeavors brought concentration of power in the hands of a few privileged individuals, and special private interests seemed to control the state's political institutions. Political bosses representing the lumber barons or railroad magnates controlled the state legislators as well as congressmen and senators in Washington. The system worked for the benefit of many but in its smoothly running operations, democracy itself appeared to be threatened. Railroads and other big business enjoyed immunity from heavy taxation, and graft and corruption permeated political life on every level. Wisconsin's response, in the form of the Progressive movement, focused worldwide attention on the Badger State and on its leader, Robert M. La Follette.

In a sense, the progressive impulse was an attempt to return to a simpler, less complicated era. Its spokesmen challenged the special interest groups with the enthusiasm and vigor of crusaders against the powerful forces of evil. It involved a clear-cut return to morality, a morality which was viewed in terms of the good old days when the basic values of the American agrarians were taken for granted. And in the process of erecting a practical political program the Progressives themselves learned that in order to cope successfully with the evils they deplored they too would have to compromise their ideals at times, establish a machine-like organization, and deal with the ambitions for increased power among some of their own leaders.

By 1900 things in Wisconsin were ripe for a change, but in many ways the setting differed only in degree from the scene of the previous decades. Dairy farming continued to be an unusually practicable and profitable operation and Wisconsin dairymen applied the new scientific knowledge they obtained from University short courses and agricultural college bulletins to improve the quality of their products and the efficiency of their farms. Wisconsin quickly became the nation's leading dairy state. As new and unforeseen problems arose the dairy interests, often in collaboration with the University, set out to tackle them. An excellent illustration of the manner in which this was done was the fight against bovine tuberculosis. Dean H. L. Russell of the College of Agriculture led the way in a voluntary crusade against the disease, and after his point was made and most dairymen agreed to take action, laws were passed that further encouraged progress. In 1915 the state began to accredit dairy herds that had been thoroughly tested and proved healthy. Two years later a Live Stock Sanitary Board worked out a plan for compulsory testing if 51 per cent of the cattle owners in a stated area agreed. Wisconsin's method succeeded in wiping out the disease, and the state's reputation for excellent dairy products was well known in Chicago and the other national markets farther away.

Although each year an increasing number of Wisconsin farmers became dairymen, there were still many others who carried on a more diversified type of farming, growing such crops as wheat, corn, oats, hay, barley, potatoes, peas, sugar beets, tobacco, and soy beans. Science also gave new weapons to these farmers in their never-ending struggle against the plant diseases and insects which plagued their efforts to continue agricultural pursuits in a world of rapid change. Eventually they had to adapt themselves to some of the changes over which they had little or no control. When automobiles and tractors began to replace the horse, many Wisconsin farmers turned from horse breeding to poultry raising.

Such a change in the emphasis of farming sometimes brought in a time of prosperity for the individuals involved, but others seemed to prosper less than they had before. The percentage of Wisconsin farmers who were tenants rather than owners of the land they worked rose from 9.1 per cent in 1880 to 14.4 per cent in 1920, yet the increase in tenancy on Wisconsin farms was less than in the nation at large. Not all of those had dropped down the agricultural ladder from owners to tenants. Some tenants farmed lands that others had purchased on an investment, and some eventually acquired titles to farms of their own.

Despite good prices for agricultural products, farmers were convinced that the middlemen—the sellers and processors—between them and the city consumers acquired the lion's share of profit. They also voiced strong complaints about the excessive cost of seed, fertilizer, feed, and other items essential to their work. As the farmers saw it, monopolies controlled the prices and victimized the purchasers. A possible solution was the creation of various co-operative business ventures.

Consumers' or buying co-operatives began in England in the 1840's and after a period of successful growth spread to Scandinavia and other parts of Europe. The Grange and other farm organizations in the United States promoted the co-operative idea but most of the buyers' co-operatives failed for one reason or another. Around 1910 immigrants from Finland and Bohemia, with a knowledge of successful Old World consumer co-operative techniques, began arriving in Wisconsin and some other midwestern states. The Finns were especially active in starting and supporting co-operative stores and by 1917 they had contributed to the development of a strong consumer co-operative movement in Wisconsin. Most of the co-operative stores were in smaller towns and villages and their total amount of business was considerable. The stores purchased goods through the Central Co-operative Wholesale in Superior which became the largest co-operative wholesale business in the country. In 1917 its annual sales exceeded $25,000 and by 1935 the figure had risen to more than $2,000,000.

Besides purchasing groceries, farm supplies, and other items through co-operative stores or buying associations, Wisconsin farmers also joined together in producers' or marketing co-operatives. Earlier ventures in this field had also led to failure, loss of precious savings and disillusionment with the co-operative idea. But shortly after the turn of the century a new farm organization, the American Society of Equity, revived the idea and promoted some highly successful co-operatives of both the buying and marketing variety. In 1906 Wisconsin cranberry growers organized the American Cranberry Exchange, the first large scale commodity marketing association. Three years later Door County fruit farmers founded another successful co-operative, the Door County Fruit Growers Union. Eventually Wisconsin farmers sold tobacco, livestock, milk, sugar beets, and other products through their own marketing associations.

Besides benefitting from the experience of some European immigrants and the support of various farm organizations, Wisconsin's co-operatives received assistance from the state. The model legislation of 1911 was merely one of a series of friendly laws encouraging the formation of co-operatives. The State Board of Public Affairs supplied marketing data to agricultural producers and influenced cheese manufacturers to organize the National Cheese Producers Federation. After 1919 a Division of Markets in the State Department of Agriculture provided information and lent support to the co-operative movement of Wisconsin farmers and processors. With such encouragement the co-operatives thrived; eventually there were more than a thousand consumer and producer co-operatives in the state.

At a time of rapid economic growth Wisconsin industry also fared well. The percentage of business failures in Wisconsin was smaller than in the nation as a whole and a number of new industries supplemented the older ones. By 1923 the state led the nation in the production of certain types of heavy machinery including concrete mixers, ore crushers, dredging and excavating equipment. The manufacturing of aluminum products, industrial appliances, and farm machinery gave work to additional thousands. The appearance of automobiles signalled new industrial opportunities and Wisconsin became an important producer of motor vehicles. Not all of Wisconsin's workers were engaged in large manufacturing concerns; about half of them worked in small industries which produced such varied items as mattresses, musical instruments, refrigerators, boats, stoves, and luggage. Some of the manufacturing was closely allied to Wisconsin's agricultural pursuits. Numerous creameries and cheese factories scattered throughout the state produced the quality product that eventually gave Wisconsin a reputation as America's Dairyland.

At the same time that many dairy farmers prospered in the older, settled portions of Wisconsin, some others staked out claims to land in the northern, cutover counties. Those who promoted the idea of settling the cutover lands changed their tactics after 1900. Disappointment and frustration with the difficulties of attempting to farm stump-ridden land had caused many of the earlier settlers to abandon their claims and leave the area. As a result

The Cutover, northern Wisconsin
Library of Congress Photo

the land companies began to supply more specific information about the region and its usefulness. Some extended credit to carefully selected and informed settlers, and furnished the use of farm and stump-removing machinery at low cost. Promoters like Benjamin F. Faast, who organized several land companies, advertised the region, but called attention to the shortcomings as well as the advantages of life in northern Wisconsin. The new promotional technique brought some tangible results. James L. "Stumpland" Gates, a large-scale speculator, claimed that he sold 456,000 acres for more than $2,000,-000 in the years from 1898 to 1902.

The state also provided aid to the northern settlers. Harry L. Russell, Dean of the College of Agriculture, spoke and wrote in favor of settling the cutover land. Some of the land was free of taxes for three years if farmers settled and worked on it. After scientists had proved

TNT useful and safe for removing stumps, the College of Agriculture distributed several million pounds of the powerful explosive to northern settlers. Later, the University provided soil surveys and economic inventories to give guidance to the farmers.

However, intelligent and discriminating promotion and state aid were not enough to attract a flood of settlers to the cutover region of northern Wisconsin. Those who went there cleared nearly a million acres between 1900 and 1920, yet most of the land remained in stumps and unsettled. When newcomers arrived they usually chose to settle in the southern fringe of counties but even there less than 30 per cent of the land had actually been cultivated by 1920. In the southern section, too, many settlers left rather than continue trying to work land that was not fit for farming. The unhappy experiences of many who had tried to farm the northern counties led a large number of people to listen to those writers and conservationists who favored reforestation rather than settlement of the northern cutover lands.

During the period of the organization of farm co-operatives, rising industrialization, and increased settlement of the cutover lands, a majority of Wisconsin voters were turning to Progressivism. Despite the relative prosperity of Wisconsin farmers and industrialists in this period, there was still good reason for dissatisfaction. The Progressive movement appealed to those who sought honest government and moderate economic reforms in the interest of public morality and democracy. Among the dissatisfied were farmers and lumbermen who continued to complain about the high freight rates of railroad companies who appeased politicians and public leaders by giving them free passes. The free pass evil became a symbol of the prevalent corruption which permeated state politics. State Assemblyman Albert R. Hall gained renown for his persistent fight to stop the practice of giving free passes. In the process he stirred up opposition within the Republican Party. Republican factional disputes became even more acute when Henry C. Payne, influential chairman of the state committee, irritated the farmers by lobbying, both in Madison and Washington, for the hated oleomargarine interest. Isaac Stephenson, millionaire lumberman, disgruntled because he was not made sena-

UPPER CAMPUS FROM LIBRARY.

University of Wisconsin
SHSW Colls.

tor in 1899, threw his support and his money on the side
of the young reform faction of the Republican Party. By
then the state's political leaders were becoming painfully
aware of the demands for reform, and the legislature
passed an inheritance tax, an anti-lobbying law, and a
corrupt practices act. But these laws met only a few of the
numerous demands made by the reform group within the
Republican Party; the reformers wanted much more than
that and ultimately, under the leadership of La Follette
and other Progressives, they were determined to get them.

La Follette and his followers sought to bring an end to
bossism and the corrupt alliance between big business

Wisconsin state Capitol
SHSW Colls.

and government which they believed had made a mockery
of democracy. Their crusade was one phase of a national progressive reaction, but in Wisconsin La Follette,
his ideas and personality, gave a unique twist to the
movement. Born on a Dane County farm in 1855, La Follette was conscientious and hard working even though he
seldom enjoyed good health. He worked his way through
the University of Wisconsin where he fell under the spell
of President Bascom and his idealism, which included an
unselfish devotion to serving the state. Years later La
Follette claimed that all of his accomplishments had
grown out of the inspiration he acquired at the Univer-

sity. It was there, a year before he entered as a freshman, that he heard Edward G. Ryan tell the graduating law class, "for the first time really in our politics money is taking the field as an organized power." As a student at Madison, La Follette thought deeply about the problem Ryan had spelled out and there he strengthened the will to do something about it. More important than his course work was "the spirit of the institution—a high spirit of earnest endeavor, a spirit of fresh interest in new things, and beyond all else a sense that somehow the state and the university were intimately related, and that they should be of mutual service."

It was at the University, too, that young Bob La Follete learned the significance of facts. He respected the scholarship of his renowned professors and he realized that their reputation as scholars resulted directly from their painstaking digging in the library for facts. Later, when he became Dane County's district attorney, La Follette also emphasized the importance of looking at all available evidence. "Facts," he said in his autobiography, "count everywhere. Whether the matter in hand is railroad legislation or the tariff, it is always a question of digging out the facts upon which to base your case."

The Midwestern heritage of agrarian protest also influenced La Follette. He knew firsthand the hardships and uncertainties of farm life, and it was in moral terms that he contrasted the "grasping" monopolists and the toiling farmer. Reading a dog-eared copy of one of Henry George's books confirmed his sentiments. As a youth he had heard and felt the stirring of the Granger movement. He never forgot its deep indignation nor its ineffective attempt to bring the state political apparatus to bear upon the monopolies and railroads. La Follette was an agrarian and Wisconsin farmers formed the backbone

Robert Marion La Follette
SHSW Colls.

of his political faction during the early phase of the Progressive movement.

Curiously, there was little in the beginning of La Follette's political career to hint at his later zeal for reform. After graduating from the University, he studied law and was admitted to the bar. In 1880 he entered politics as candidate for district attorney in Dane County. He was persistent and determined in his political ambitions and he won the office without the support of some of the older Republican Party leaders. In 1884 voters from the Second District sent him to Congress where he loyally supported party measures along with other Republicans until 1890 when a Democratic victory swept him out of office. In Washington, Senator Philetus Sawyer befriended the young representative, overlooking his independent and somewhat unpredictable nature. But in 1891 La Follette clashed with Sawyer in a way that could not be ignored.

The dispute grew out of the treasury cases which the Democrats were pushing in order to discredit the former Republican administrations. As bondsman for several former treasurers, Sawyer stood to lose as much as $200,000 should the cases go against them. After a meeting between La Follette and Sawyer in Milwaukee's Plankinton House La Follette charged that Sawyer had tried to bribe him to influence the presiding judge, Robert G. Siebecker, La Follette's brother-in-law and former law partner. La Follette's statement led to denials and counter-charges by Sawyer and his powerful friends, and the controversy provided exciting newspaper copy. What started as a clash between two personalities soon developed into a rift in the Republican Party, with Sawyer representing the old boss-politicians and La Follette the young reformer-politicians.

In 1894 the La Follette Republicans tried without success to nominate Nils P. Haugen for governor and two years later, La Follette himself. Convinced that he had

La Follette campaigning
SHSW Colls.

been cheated out of the nomination in 1896, La Follette began in earnest his crusade against bossism. He was now determined to redeem completely the "good State of Wisconsin" from the rule of "a handful of men who had destroyed every vestige of democracy in the commonwealth. They settled in private conferences practically all nominations for important offices, controlled conventions, dictated legislation, and had even sought to lay corrupt hands on the courts of justice," said La Follette in retrospect.

The reform faction gradually grew in power with each

passing state convention. Although it was not influential enough to nominate La Follette in 1898, its strength was sufficient to have a number of reform measures included in the state platform. Finally in 1900 La Follette won the Republican nomination. La Follette's nomination was unanimous, receiving the support of the stalwarts as well as the reformers among Wisconsin Republicans. The contest became known as the "Harmony Campaign," conducted against Louis G. Bomrich, the Democratic candidate. Isaac "Uncle Ike" Stephenson, a lumber-baron politician temporarily turned reformer, paid many of the campaign bills and he later underwrote the pro-La Follette *Milwaukee Free Press.*

La Follette conducted a hard-hitting and effective campaign. He had once given serious consideration to a career on the stage and he transferred his dramatic abilities to the spotlight of the political hustings. During the course of his speeches, often made from a farm wagon, "Fightin' Bob" would remove his coat and open his shirt collar, while his message would be transmitted in varying volumes ranging from an angry shout to an almost inaudible whisper. His timing was superb and his speeches usually brought forth strong cheers and positive approval from his listeners.

Despite his support from the Old Guard, candidate La Follette gave emphasis to the need for reform in his many speeches, most of which were a variation on his "Menace of the Machine" address, which he had delivered at the University of Chicago three years earlier. In the fall of 1900 he traveled more than 6,000 miles and delivered 216 speeches to an estimated 200,000 listeners in 61 Wisconsin counties. He bore down hardest on the issues of the direct primary and more effective railroad legislation. When the votes were in, La Follette received 264,419 to his opponent's 160,674.

During La Follette's first term as Wisconsin governor the anti-La Follette Republicans or "stalwarts" controlled the state senate and effectively prevented the adoption of any major reform measures. But in time the La Follette faction grew and after three terms as governor the progressive reformer could look back upon a notable record of achievement. After a stiff fight the legislature passed the primary election law of 1903, with the proviso that it first pass the test of a popular referendum. The voters approved the primary idea and their endorsement removed the selection of all state candidates from the direct control of party bosses. Under La Follette's leadership Wisconsin got effective railroad regulation under a commission which also had power to control other types of public utilities, a thoroughgoing civil service program, corrupt practices and anti-lobbying laws, and a workmen's compensation law. The legislature chose La Follette as senator in 1905 but he delayed going to Washington a year in order to complete the reform program he had pledged his supporters during the campaign of 1904.

Progressivism was only beginning in Wisconsin. La Follette went to Washington with the full support of a smoothly-running political faction behind him and with subordinates steeped in the program of Progressivism and sufficiently competent in the business of politics to continue his reform program in the state. As senator, La Follette tried to introduce the idea of progressive reform on a national basis. At first he was alone but soon a small group of "insurgent" Republicans assisted him in his fight for more effective railroad regulation, the direct election of senators, and laws providing for improved working conditions for seamen and railroad workers.

It was his Wisconsin career and his success in the state that made La Follette the symbol of Progressive reform throughout the nation. In Wisconsin he developed the techniques and ideas with which people everywhere associated him. The state became an experiment in progressive government. The Wisconsin Idea, as it came to be called, involved efficient government controlled by the voters and the use of specialized experts in the interest of the state.

The University of Wisconsin played a significant part in the reform. La Follette was its first graduate to become governor, and University President Charles R. Van Hise was its first graduate student to receive a Ph.D. degree. Van Hise favored an extension of the services of the University to all of the people of the state. Under his administration and with the goading of Charles McCarthy of the Legislative Reference Library the Extension Division came to life. Louis E. Reber accepted an invitation to come to Wisconsin from Pennsylvania State College and build up the division. William H. Lighty developed a program of correspondence courses for teachers and other state residents who could not attend classes during the regular term.

President Van Hise encouraged his faculty to serve the state as consultants to legislative committees, assistants in drafting laws, and members of various commissions. Professor John R. Commons helped draft the bill which created the Industrial Commission and he later served as a member of the commission. T. S. Adams assisted in framing the state income tax law and he too served on the tax commission. There were many others. By 1912 Charles McCarthy could list forty-six men who had combined teaching in the University with noteworthy service to the state. A Saturday Lunch Club brought scholars and legislators together weekly to exchange ideas and information. One observer commented: "The University of Wisconsin has become a kind of 'consulting engineer' in the public life of the State . . ." and William Ellery

Leonard, poet on the University faculty, spoke about the "twin domes of law and learning" located a mile apart on Madison's State Street.

No less than State Street as a connecting link between the two institutions was Charles McCarthy, who joined the staff of the Free Library Commission after earning his doctorate in history at the University. McCarthy was equally persistent in his efforts for more scientific and efficient government and for enlarged educational opportunities for the people of Wisconsin. He believed a state university "should serve the state and all of its people" and he worked assiduously to promote the program of extension work of the University and continuation and vocational schools in the state. In 1901 the legislature established the Legislative Reference Library, a unique institution created to assist the legislators in their search for facts on which to base improved laws. The new venture grew out of the Free Library Commission; it was partly the idea of the commission's executive secretary, Frank A. Hutchins, and partly McCarthy's.

McCarthy became the first librarian of the Legislative Reference Library. He provided fast and efficient service and the library furnished trained research talent as well as books and documents. In 1907 McCarthy added a bill-drafting service to the library's features. Critics derided it as McCarthy's "bill factory," but this and other innovations of the Wisconsin Progressives favorably impressed countless Americans throughout the nation. In 1912 Americans read two books which described the progressive state: Charles McCarthy's *The Wisconsin Idea,* and Frederic C. Howe's *Wisconsin: An Experiment in Democracy. La Follette's Autobiography* appeared the following year. All of them stressed the pragmatic, trial-and-error spirit of the Wisconsin Idea.

The Progressives constantly emphasized the spirit of

good government rather than any preconceived plan or abstract solution. They met each problem as it came along instead of imposing rigid principles upon governmental procedure. And the method worked to give efficient service and good government to what had been a graft-ridden state. Wisconsin's Industrial Commission became a model institution. The law creating it provided for maximum co-operation with all interests involved and gave the commission generous leeway in defining safe working conditions for various industries. The fair mindedness of the members and the value of such intelligent regulation usually brought full and complete co-operation from both management and labor, making coercion seldom necessary. In other areas new problems were met in a similar spirit. Whether the issue was more equitable distribution of the tax burden, the protection of public health, the need to protect farmers from monopoly practices of wholesale buyers, or laws regulating working conditions in factories, the Progressive program made Wisconsin a leader as a service state. The spirit of Progressivism was as significant a part of the program as any law or regulation. La Follette maintained that the Progressive movement had succeeded "if it can be shown that Wisconsin is a happier state to live in, that its institutions are more democratic, that the opportunities of all its people are more equal, that social justice more nearly prevails, [and] that human life is safer and sweeter."

But by no means were all of the progressive achievements La Follette's. Wisconsin Progressivism began with the support of a small faction within the Republican Party. As the faction grew in strength it drew support from the farmers, some businessmen, journalists, professional people, and politicians. There were factions within the faction and some of them had important leaders of their own, like James O. "Yim" Davidson, who was very influential in enlisting the Wisconsin Norwegians in the Progressive camp. Davidson served two terms as lieutenant governor under La Follette, and became governor in January, 1906, when La Follette resigned to accept a place in the United States Senate. In the fall primary elections La Follette threw his support to Irvine L. Lenroot rather than to Davidson. Despite La Follette's opposition, Davidson won the Republican primary and was elected governor.

Davidson had sufficient political strength of his own to challenge La Follette successfully and win a nomination for governor in 1906 against his opposition. By 1905 the Progressive faction was the most powerful in the Wisconsin Republican Party, but with the passing years the elements which composed the group shifted and changed. Two significant groups that had not lent support to the Progressives in the early phase of the movement became important later. They were the Germans, who favored only certain parts of the Progressive program, and organized labor.

The complex program associated with Wisconsin progressive reform required the efforts and support of many legislators and politicians other than La Follette. James O. Davidson, Francis E. McGovern, Irvine L. Lenroot, Herman L. Ekern, and many others made substantial contributions to the reform impulse which is so often associated solely with La Follette's name. During Davidson's terms as governor, from January, 1906, to January, 1911, considerable significant progressive legislation was enacted, including laws providing for state control of corporation stock issues, an extension of the power of the railroad commission, a fixing of railroad fares, and stricter regulation of insurance companies. Governor Davidson's successor, Francis E. McGovern, also served two terms and further implemented the Progressive program by supporting legislation establishing a workable state income tax, workers' compensation, regulation of labor of women and children, encouraging co-operatives, and limiting corrupt political practices. Together, the Davidson and McGovern administrations added a substantial body of progressive legislation to those Wisconsin laws which had been passed earlier under La Follette.

Irvine L. Lenroot, as speaker of the state assembly from 1903 to 1906, gave valuable support to Governor La Follette when critical legislation like the primary election law was under consideration. Another key person, Herman L. Ekern, also served in the state assembly where he helped write acts providing retirement benefits for railroad workers and teachers, and diligently promoted the creation of Wisconsin's model life insurance code. He later served as insurance commissioner and from 1923 to 1927 as state attorney general.

Sometimes quarrels within the ranks of Wisconsin's Progressives prevented the passage of important legislation. In 1913 factionalism made it impossible to pass a marketing commission bill which many of the Progressives favored. The bill provided for a number of important aids to farmers and had the support of the Wisconsin Society of Equity, La Follette, and most of the Progressive leaders. But it also had the support of Governor Francis E. McGovern, with whom La Follette had broken after he had supported the presidential candidacy of Theodore Roosevelt in 1912. It was opposition to McGovern that killed the desirable bill. Progressive legislators who were loyal to La Follette feared that so popular a measure might further strengthen McGovern as a political leader in the state. After the legislature had turned down the bill one pro-La Follette state senator explained to Charles McCarthy that he would continue to aid progressive legislation as he had in the past, but only when it came "from a source that is *not objectionable* to a majority in Wisconsin." When dealing with the realities and exigencies of everyday politics the Progressives sometimes found it necessary to use methods that dangerously resembled those of the old-style politicians.

La Follette's followers hoped that his leadership would provide the cohesive force necessary to hold the various Progressive factions together, especially after the Direct Primary Law, which they had so ardently promoted, had made old-style bossism ineffective. The primary, after all, could work for one faction of the party as well as for another. It was a potential threat to any political faction, in-

---

TWO OPINIONS OF ROBERT M. LA FOLLETTE

Senator La Follette became one of the most famous and controversial figures of Wisconsin history. In 1924, Frank Kent, an observer for the Democratic Baltimore SUN, *reported:*

"He (La Follette) is the 'Old Guard' in Wisconsin. He is the boss out here, and his machine, when you scrape off the camouflage, is the old-style political machine, run in the old-style political way and for the old-style political purposes—namely, to keep him and his friends in power.

He keeps firm control over the Republican primaries, holds fast to the Republican party label and nominates his candidates. From the Governor of the state down the line to the justices of the peace, the jobs in Wisconsin are filled with La Follette machine workers. . . . The fact is that La Follette's grip on the state is a strong one. It is not possible under present circumstances to beat him . . . and his control over the state legislature is supreme."—EDWARD N. DOAN, *The La Follettes and the Wisconsin Idea* (New York, 1947), 113.

---

cluding La Follette's. Although he was sensitive to possible criticism as a new-style boss, La Follette used such well-established political practices as patronage, distribution of favors, and punishment of dissenters to maintain control of the party. The diligent support of Governor La Follette by the state game wardens led one editor to suggest that they were "strolling around the state . . . hunting for men who will vote for La Follette at the next state convention." La Follette also gave some of his partisans jobs as inspectors of illuminating oils; the state treasurer's report for 1904 included the names of eighty-two oil inspectors, whose total salaries and expenses totaled more than $20,000.

La Follette's opponents were quick to label him another boss, and they began to talk and write about the dangers of "La Follettism." Some referred to him as "Iago" La Follette, calling attention to his flair for the dramatic which first came out as a student at the University when he won an oratory contest on the subject of Shakespeare's famous character.

Although La Follette was the most powerful single Progressive political leader in the state, he was never able to gain complete control over the Republican Party or of the state itself. The Progressive era was a time of contention and strife in politics and even after the so-called "Harmony Campaign" of 1900 which brought La Follette into the capitol at Madison, disunity was characteristic of the Republicans. In 1901 anti-La Follette Republicans organized the Republican League of Wisconsin, or the Eleventh Story League, so-called because of its headquarters on the eleventh floor of Milwaukee's Hermann building. Three years later a stalwart bolt at the state convention in the University gymnasium at Madison involved the Progressives in some high-handed tactics and took some of the leading Republicans temporarily out of the party. As a party leader La Follette demanded complete loyalty from his subordinates, and proved to be difficult to please. At one time or another during his political career he quarreled and broke with a number in the Progressive camp, including James O. Davidson, Francis McGovern, Irvine Lenroot, William H. Hatton, and Isaac Stephenson. While undoubtedly the divisions in the Progressive ranks were caused by a number of factors and were not all the responsibility of La Follette, his leadership was incapable of holding the group together and preventing such factional splits.

La Follette did not always succeed in dominating the Wisconsin Progressives. He was not able to prevent the election of Davidson as governor in 1906, nor Isaac Stephenson's election to the Senate. Francis E. McGovern had long been a threat to La Follette because of the strong personal following he had in Milwaukee. Despite La Follette's threat to punish McGovern for supporting Theodore Roosevelt in 1912, McGovern succeeded in being nominated and winning another term as governor. During World War I, when a vacancy occurred because of Senator Husting's death in 1917, La Follette supported James Thompson, who was defeated in the primaries by Irvine L. Lenroot, a prowar Progressive who had opposed La Follette's criticism of the war. But within the divisive ranks of Wisconsin's Republicans, La Follette led an important faction from the time he became governor until his death in 1925.

The same dramatic ability that provided fuel for those who tried to fan the fires of hatred against La Follette and his ideas, enabled him to reach the mass of voters in the state. His lengthy and dramatic orations held the attention of thousands who were thrilled with his crusading zeal for good government and against the wicked power of big business. And he made the most of any issue. As governor, he dramatically read his own messages to the legislators and also took occasion to scold them when they refused to endorse parts of his reform program. When he wanted a legislature friendly to his policies he exposed the voting records of legislators on key Progressive issues. The "roll call" method of campaigning worked. His opponents charged that La Follette wanted only submissive legislators but friends justified the tactic, pointing out the need for progressive legislators if the program was to continue.

La Follette was a man of strong personal ambition who tended to equate his own program with the public interest. He was convinced that if the voters only knew the facts and understood the issues they would certainly support his struggle for morality in government. He was exceptionally imaginative in driving home the point. When the same legislature that had turned down a stronger railroad tax passed a law taxing dogs, he vetoed the dog tax, claiming it was unfair to tax poor farmers' dogs while wealthy railroad corporations paid only a small amount of their fair share.

TERMS OF WISCONSIN'S GOVERNORS, 1901–1927

January, 1901–1906   Robert M. La Follette
January, 1906–1911   James O. Davidson
January, 1911–1915   Francis E. McGovern
January, 1915–1921   Emanuel L. Philipp
January, 1921–1927   John J. Blaine
    —*Wisconsin Blue Book*, 1927 (Madison, 1927), 88.

Bob La Follette was not a radical. He had no blueprint for the perfect society; his ideas and methods were rooted in the American pragmatic tradition. He was careful, too, to calculate the political effects of the issues he supported. He did not favor disrupting the economy or substituting anything else for the capitalist economic system. Many of his reforms were moderate and thus acceptable to a large number of people including certain businessmen who, for one reason or another, supported him and the Progressive program. Before his election as governor in 1900 La Follette met with Marvin Hughitt, president of the Chicago and North Western Railroad, and assured him that any regulatory measure he obtained would be fair and just to the railroads. The Wisconsin railroad commission occasionally raised as well as lowered the rates. Uncle "Ike" Stephenson came into La Follette's camp in part because of his traditional lumber baron's dislike of the "old railroad-corporation crowd, the inner ring which controlled party affairs to the exclusion of all others." Then, when the railroad crowd had been put in its place and some good laws passed, Stephenson thought the Progressive movement had performed its function and he left its ranks for "stalwart" Republicanism again. "There the task ended for me," he commented.

But not for "Fightin' Bob," whose struggle was continuous and whose political ambition seemed to observers to have no limits. From time to time he emphasized several issues to the exclusion of others, but he always kept in mind the spirit of the crusade. To him it was a perpetual struggle, an unceasing warfare against the special privilege system. He also had ambitions to lead the nation in the same crusade that had redeemed Wisconsin from bossism and corruption. In order to further this ambition and to provide a vehicle for progressive opinion, he founded *La Follette's Magazine* in 1909. Both in 1908 and 1912 he attempted to get the Republican presidential nomination, and in 1912 he lost out only when Theodore Roosevelt threw his ten-gallon hat into the ring as the Progressive candidate for the Republican nomination. Roosevelt also claimed to be a Progressive, though in 1908 he had privately referred to "the La Follette type of fool radicalism." When Roosevelt failed to win the nomination he temporarily left the party and ran on the Progressive or Bull Moose ticket. All of the platforms borrowed heavily from La Follette's program and some Americans believed with him that their most famous progressive leader had been grossly cheated of the nomination. It was not until after World War I that La Follette had a chance to carry his message to all the people of the nation.

The war brought temporary havoc to an already troubled Wisconsin Progressive movement. In 1914 two

Progressives and a stalwart competed for the Wisconsin gubernatorial nomination in the primary, and the stalwart won. As a result of the Progressive split, Emanuel L. Philipp, a wealthy owner of a refrigerator car transit company, became governor of Wisconsin and served three terms which covered the war years. Philipp campaigned on the issue of lower taxes and less interference in the affairs of the people by the state university. But after assuming office the stalwarts gradually came to accept a part of the Progressive program. Most of the major reforms were allowed to stand and Governor Philipp even made peace with the University. The stalwart victory represented in part a reaction to "La Follettism" and the stalwart faction kept control of the party until 1920.

The period of stalwart supremacy stemmed in part from La Follette's opposition to the War. After the European war broke out in 1914 La Follette strongly supported the neutrality statements of the Wilson administration. Like many other Americans, he felt that the war was not America's affair and that entering it would only further enrich the wealthy monopolists and munitions manufacturers. As the national administration became less and less neutral in its attitude, La Follette came to lead the opposition to the drift toward war. When in 1916 President Wilson tried to kill a congressional resolution warning Americans against traveling on armed merchant ships, Senator La Follette labeled it "interference" and maintained that "Democratic control of foreign policy is a basic principle of all organized effort looking for the future establishment of permanent world peace." When La Follette led the filibuster against a proposed administration bill to arm American merchantmen on the high seas, Wilson lashed into that "little band of willful men who represent no opinion except their own." And when the vote on war came, La Follette and five other senators, along with fifty congressmen, nine of them from Wisconsin, voted "no." He opposed the military conscription bill and the severe Espionage Act, which he charged seriously endangered the American tradition of freedom of expression. He also led an unsuccessful movement to shift the financial burden of the war to big business. For La Follette the war was no excuse for stopping the ongoing Progressive movement, but the nation at large was involved too emotionally with war fervor to listen to his voice.

La Follette met with little but criticism for his stand on the war. The Wisconsin state senate censured him, the Madison Club expelled him, and newspapers accused him of such high crimes as sedition, disloyalty, and treason. In a speech at Racine, Theodore Roosevelt said, "I abhor the Hun without our gates, but more I abhor the Hun within our gates." When La Follette delivered a speech in St. Paul in which he said that America had grievances against Germany, the Associated Press misquoted him as saying that we had "no" grievances against Germany. Although a minority of Americans including some of Wisconsin's Germans applauded La Follette, even many of his former friends and political supporters deserted him. University students in Madison hanged him in effigy and all but a handful of the faculty severely condemned him in a widely publicized round robin letter. Even though criticized by such close associates as Charles McCarthy, President Van Hise, and John R. Commons, La Follette would not modify his words nor tone down his opposition. While millions of Americans condemned him for what they believed to be highly irresponsible statements, others considered him a courageous man who defended something precious in the American tradition, the right to dissent. After the war ended, many more came to feel that way.

La Follette's wartime acts, the large German popula-

Trucks for the Army, made in Wisconsin
SHSW Colls.

tion, and Milwaukee's Socialist administration brought a great deal of unwanted attention to the Badger State. Cynics ridiculed it as a "58 per cent state" and writers frequently referred to its war record in insulting language. The University students and faculty and many others in Wisconsin protested this unfair accusation.

Actually, Wisconsin did not oppose the war. The great majority of its citizens joined the nation in its crusade to make the world safe for democracy. Business, labor, and the farmers all enjoyed high prosperity during the lush times. The complaints of some dairy farmers because their prices did not rise as rapidly as prices of feed and other items they had to buy were hardly heard amid the enthusiastic speeches for loyalty. A national draft official commented, "I have come to expect the impossible from Wisconsin." After inspecting the state organizations of de-

Sending the boys off to war
SHSW Colls.

fense, Ray Stannard Baker reported, "You have in Wisconsin the best organized and the most efficient, the most constructive, and the most far-seeing defense league of any of the states I have visited." Wisconsin National Guardsmen in the Thirty-second or Red Arrow Division soon gained a reputation for fearless and effective fighting. *"Les Terribles,"* the French called them and others of the division.

Wisconsin was the first state to organize a State Council of Defense and the Wisconsin Idea for war contributed a number of nationally accepted practices, including meatless and wheatless days, to the war effort. Even though the Socialist Party refused to support the war, the

Drilling at Camp Douglas
SHSW Colls.

Food Conservation display

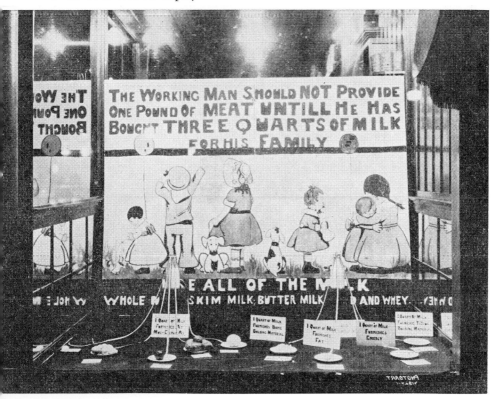

Socialist mayor of Milwaukee participated in preparedness parades, rendered full co-operation with the draft and established a Milwaukee council of defense at the same time that he defended the right of opposition voices, like that of Victor Berger, to be heard. In short, Wisconsin's war program was an extension of its domestic progressive program. The same efficiency and good administration which had characterized the earlier reform was then applied to the problems of a state at war. And when the war was over and some of the people began to wonder what it had all been about, they once again turned to the Progressive leadership of Robert M. La Follette and his followers.

The war affected life in many ways in Wisconsin and the changes that took place usually met with varied reaction. Two of the more important by-products of the war were prohibition and woman suffrage. Temperance and prohibition had been a factor in Wisconsin politics from time to time ever since the 1850's, when Yankee reformers clashed with German immigrants on the issue. During World War I the state's legislature went along reluctantly with ratification of the Eighteenth Amendment, partly because to do otherwise would have appeared truckling to the German interests and opposed to the idea of conserving foodstuffs. Wisconsin breweries led the opposition to prohibition and their pronouncements proved to be popular with many in the state. During prohibition most of the brewing companies turned to the manufacture of candy, malt, chewing gum, near-beer, and similar products. In several Wisconsin elections the people voted on special questions associated with the Eighteenth Amendment. In 1926, by a referendum decision, Wisconsin voters requested that the federal Volstead Act be modified to make beer legal, and in 1929 another referendum repealed state legislation enforcing the prohibition amendment.

When John James Blaine ran for the United States Senate in 1926 he promised to "bring back beer" if elected, and he led the movement for repeal of the unpopular amendment. In 1932 Blaine introduced the Senate resolution which resulted in repeal, with the ratification of the Twenty-first Amendment a year later.

As a reform, woman suffrage changed things less than prohibition, and soon became accepted without further opposition. Ardent suffragettes like Ada L. James, Olympia Brown, and Mrs. Belle Case La Follette had long agitated for the vote. In 1911 a Wisconsin law provided for extending suffrage to women if the matter met approval at a referendum. The zealous women held mass meetings, delivered thousands of speeches, and distributed countless pieces of literature, but the male voters overwhelmingly rejected the proposed change. The women were undaunted, however, and continued to demand the vote through the Woman Suffrage Association. By 1919 they had convinced the legislature to hold another referendum, but in the meantime the Nineteenth Amendment came before the state for action. This time Wisconsin did not drag its heels; the legislature quickly ratified the amendment and notice of its action was the first to reach Washington. After winning the suffrage, the women organized the League of Women Voters to encourage its use and to direct it toward goals the League believed desirable.

In 1920 Wisconsin returned to the Progressive Republican camp. When Governor Philipp turned down the idea of a fourth term the nomination went to John James Blaine, a follower of La Follette and also the candidate of the Nonpartisan League, a farmer protest organization which had first appeared in North Dakota. Blaine won the election and served as governor until 1926, when he became a United States senator. During Blaine's six years in

the governor's office the legislature added a number of
laws in the realm of economic and social legislation, reformed the tax structure, and created a department of
markets. State constitutional amendments gave more
home rule to cities and made possible the recall of elected
officials by popular referendum. The program of the
Wisconsin Idea was resumed at home once again, but increasingly the people of Wisconsin and of the nation
turned their attention to Senator La Follette and his struggle for Progressive ideas in foreign policy and domestic
reform on the national scene.

In the Senate La Follette opposed the Versailles Treaty
and American membership in the League of Nations. He
thought the treaty was a clear violation of Wilson's

WISCONSIN'S PRESIDENTIAL VOTE, 1900–1924

1900	William McKinley, Republican	265,866
	William J. Bryan, Democrat	159,285
	John G. Wooley, Prohibition	10,027
	Eugene V. Debs, Social Democratic	7,048
	Joseph F. Malloney, Socialist Labor	503
1904	Theodore Roosevelt, Republican	280,164
	Alton B. Parker, Democrat	124,036
	Eugene V. Debs, Social Democratic	28,240
	Silas S. Swallow, Prohibition	9,770
	Thomas E. Watson, Populist	530
	Charles H. Corrigan, Socialist Labor	223
1908	William H. Taft, Republican	247,747
	William J. Bryan, Democrat	166,632
	Eugene V. Debs, Social Democratic	28,164
	Eugene W. Chafin, Prohibition	11,565
	August Gilhaus, Socialist Labor	314

1912	Woodrow Wilson, Democrat	164,228
	William H. Taft, Republican	130,695
	Theodore Roosevelt, Progressive	62,460
	Eugene V. Debs, Social Democratic	33,476
	Eugene W. Chafin, Prohibition	8,584
	A. E. Reiner, Socialist Labor	632
1916	Charles E. Hughes, Republican	220,237
	Woodrow Wilson, Democrat	191,952
	Allan Benson, Socialist	27,631
	J. Frank Hanly, Prohibition	7,318
1920	Warren G. Harding, Republican	498,576
	James M. Cox, Democrat	113,422
	Eugene V. Debs, Socialist	80,635
	Aaron S. Watkins, Prohibition	8,647
1924	Robert M. La Follette, Progressive	453,678
	Calvin Coolidge, Republican	311,614
	John W. Davis, Democrat	69,096
	William Z. Foster, Workers	3,834
	Herman P. Faris, Prohibition	2,918

pledges, and the League a league of victors only. He opposed the four-power pact of 1921 to preserve the *status quo* in eastern Asia and the Pacific as "The Morgan Four-Power Pact," designed mostly to protect private interests. When the Supreme Court threw out Progressive labor legislation he favored severely limiting its power. As leader of the influential Progressive block in the Senate, La Follette played an important role in the investigation which exposed the Teapot Dome oil scandals that helped make the Harding Administration notorious.

In 1924 a Cleveland conference composed mostly of progressive Republicans nominated La Follette for the presidency with Montana's Burton K. Wheeler, a progressive Democrat, as his running mate. The Conference for Progressive Political Action, the Socialist Party, the railroad brotherhoods, and the American Federation of Labor all endorsed La Follette. His platform included tax reform, government ownership of railroads, lower tariff, an end to judicial review, popular election of judges, and government aid to farmers. But more important than his platform was the man himself. In Wisconsin La Follette had gained a reputation as a capable reformer by making the state a model of good government. During the war he had shown himself a man of courage by opposing those measures which he believed would make America less democratic, more militaristic, and more in the control of monopoly business. Although there was little possibility that any third party could win a national election, ill fortune in the form of ill health severely hampered any chances for election that La Follette may have had. A heart ailment made it impossible for "Fightin' Bob" to fight the way he wanted. Although Wisconsin voters gave him strong support, no other state's electoral votes were his. Nevertheless, nearly five million Americans cast their votes for the Progressive leader. La Follette paid dearly for his insurgency by being disciplined by his Republican colleagues in the Senate. Less than a year after the election La Follette died, and with his death the original, crusading phase of Wisconsin's Progressive era came to an end.

Progressive reform was basically an American middle class variety of reform. It advocated no revolution nor did it envision any fundamental change in the economic or social order. It appealed rather to those voters who favored orderly change without upsetting things too much or too quickly. It called into being honest administration and efficient government, usually at a considerably increased cost. But not all the people of Wisconsin agreed about the Progressive program. Some thought the old-time politicians were better, while still others turned to Socialism. The Progressive era of the state was also the Socialist era in Milwaukee. The two programs had different leaders and completely different vocabularies, but in many ways they were remarkably similar in practice.

In Milwaukee the laboring classes turned their attention to political action after the eight-hour-day fiasco of 1886. That year a Labor or People's Party ran John Cochrane for governor and he received more than 21,000 votes. The Labor congressional candidate, Henry Smith, Jr., won the election, only to be defeated two years later when the two traditional parties formed a fusion ticket. Labor candidates continued to run for city and state offices and in 1892 and 1894 the Populist or People's Party, under the leadership of Robert Schilling, gained much of its support from Milwaukee labor. Milwaukee Socialists helped form the Social-Democratic Party in 1897 and Milwaukee came to be the first Socialist city in the nation.

The Socialists rejected the Progressive program of government regulation of industry and advocated replacing the capitalist system with a planned economy of state-owned industries. Such a change they thought to be inevitable as the laboring class became increasingly oppressed by powerful monopoly business interests. Although they believed in a type of class warfare, the Social Democrats rejected violent revolution as a means of achieving their goal. Socialism was to come by ballots rather than bullets and in the meantime they supported such measures as improved labor legislation, health and safety measures, and more efficient administration of government.

Just as Robert La Follette was the symbol of Wisconsin Progressivism, so Victor Berger became the symbol of Milwaukee Socialism. Berger, an Austrian immigrant, was

Victor Berger
SHSW Colls.

the formulator of a program of practical political action
which, while it operated under the banner of Socialism,
was actually a variety of moderate reform. Drawing
strength from the large German element and from a
strong labor movement, Berger organized the Milwaukee
Socialists into a highly successful political organization.

For years he published both a German and an English newspaper, and on the eve of elections a voluntary "bundle brigade" distributed great quantities of free reading material to all Milwaukee homes. In their campaigning the Socialists played down theory and emphasized the need for honest government in a city which had become notorious for graft, corruption, and administrative inefficiency. "Milwaukee needs a Socialistic Housecleaning," said the Socialists in 1904. Many of the city's residents agreed and widespread disgust with the old parties along with an election which saw three parties in the running led to the Socialist victory of 1910, when Emil Seidel became mayor. The party also got most other city offices as well as a majority of seats in the city council and the county board. That fall Victor Berger went to Washington as the first Socialist congressman. Both Seidel and Berger lost in 1912 but by 1916 Milwaukee had another Socialist mayor, Daniel W. Hoan. After 1912 the Socialists never completely controlled the city government but they kept Hoan in office until 1940, when Carl Zeidler ran in a nonpartisan election and defeated him. At all times they exerted a powerful influence in making Milwaukee a model city.

In 1918 Victor Berger again won a congressional election, but the House of Representatives refused to permit him to take his seat because of his recent federal conviction under the Espionage Act. Berger had supported the anti-war statement of the 1917 Socialist Convention held in St. Louis. Although he was not a pacifist, he denounced the war as a vehicle of capitalism and imperialism. Postmaster General Albert S. Burleson barred his English language paper, *The Milwaukee Leader*, from the mails and the government prosecuted Berger along with four other Socialist Party officials for conspiracy to violate the Espionage Act. Berger never served the twenty-year prison sentence he received because when the case was appealed the Supreme Court threw out the conviction on a technical point and the government did not push another trial. Partly as a protest against such convictions and the war hysteria which had produced them, Wisconsin voters again elected Berger a congressman in a special election of 1919, but the House again refused to seat him. After a third election in 1922 his right to a Congressional seat was granted and he served as a Wisconsin representative in Washington for three successive terms.

In Milwaukee, where Berger had led the party for so long, Socialism came to be increasingly like a program of municipal reform. Berger and La Follette were able to cooperate in only a few campaigns, including the presidential campaign of 1924. Each leader saw his own program as the correct one and the Socialists, in theory at least, wanted more than the moderate reforms supported by La Follette. The Socialists would have nothing to do with the Republican Party, the parent group of the Progressives. Berger suspected that the Progressives' devotion to reform was rather weak and he labelled La Follette and his followers "Progress-ifs." Yet when actually put into operation the program of the Milwaukee Socialists was quite similar to Progressivism.

The Socialists got support from Milwaukee voters because of their efficient and honest administration, improved public health measures, outstanding traffic control system, excellent police and fire protection, fine parks and recreation program, and solvent finances, rather than because of their allegiance to the ideas of Socialism. More doctrinaire Socialists in other places called Milwaukee's program "sewer socialism." The Socialists provided a city-wide example of progressive government and at times they even de-emphasized their desire for municipally-owned utilities. Many professional people, businessmen, and others in the city's middle class continued to support a Socialist mayor because he helped give Milwaukee a reputation as the best-governed city in the United States.

The Milwaukee Socialists and the La Follette Progressives both proved by example that honest government could work on the state and local level. Theirs was a political answer to some of the problems arising from a rapidly changing society which became more highly specialized and interdependent with each passing year. Their programs seemed to prove that democratic government, utilizing the skill and learning of experts, could successfully cope with graft, corruption, and inefficiency. The Wisconsin Idea, as the phrase suggests, was a state-centered program. Wisconsin soon faced new problems which brought it more than ever under the influence of outside forces; yet even in the period of depression, war and cold war, Wisconsin helped formulate important suggestions for the new problems America faced.

SUGGESTED ADDITIONAL READING

Adolfson, Lorentz H. "A Half-Century of University Extension," in the *Wisconsin Magazine of History*, 40:99–103 (Winter, 1956–1957).

Berger, Victor L. *Voice and Pen of Victor L. Berger* (Milwaukee, 1929).

Carstensen, Vernon. *Farms or Forests: Evolution of a State Land Policy for Northern Wisconsin, 1850–1932* (Madison, 1958), 1–88.

Clark, James I. *Cutover Problems: Colonization, Depression, Reforestation* (Madison, 1956).

—————. *Wisconsin Women Fight for Suffrage* (Madison, 1956).

—————. *Robert M. La Follette and Wisconsin Progressivism* (Madison, 1956).

—————. *Robert M. La Follette: Progressive* (Madison, 1957).

—————. *The Wisconsin Labor Story* (Madison, 1956).

Current, Richard N. *Pine Logs and Politics: A Life of Philetus Sawyer, 1816–1900* (Madison, 1950).

Curti, Merle and Carstensen, Vernon. *The University of Wisconsin: A History* (2 vols., Madison, 1949), II.

Duckett, Kenneth W., ed. "Suffragettes on the Stump: Letters from the Political Equality League of Wisconsin, 1912," in the *Wisconsin Magazine of History*, 38:31–34 (Autumn, 1954).

Falk, Karen. "Public Opinion in Wisconsin during World War I," in the *Wisconsin Magazine of History*, 25:389–407 (June, 1942).

Fitzpatrick, Edward A. *McCarthy of Wisconsin* (New York, 1944).

Helgeson, Arlan. "The Wisconsin Treasury Cases," in the *Wisconsin Magazine of History*, 35:129–136 (Winter, 1951–1952).
————. *Farms in the Cutover: Agricultural Settlement in Northern Wisconsin* (Madison, 1962).

Hesseltine, William B. "Robert Marion La Follette and the Principles of Americanism," in the *Wisconsin Magazine of History*, 31:261–267 (March, 1948).

Hoan, Daniel Webster. *City Government; the Record of the Milwaukee Experiment* (New York, 1936).

Johnston, Scott D. "Wisconsin Socialists and the Conference for Progressive Political Action," in the *Wisconsin Magazine of History*, 37:96–100 (Winter, 1953–1954).

Kane, Lucile. "Settling the Wisconsin Cutovers," in the *Wisconsin Magazine of History*, 40:91–98 (Winter, 1956–1957).

Kennedy, Padraic M. "Lenroot, La Follette, and the Campaign of 1906," in the *Wisconsin Magazine of History*, 42:163–174 (Spring, 1959).

Korman, Gerd. "Political Loyalties, Immigrant Traditions, and Reform: The Wisconsin German-American Press and Progressivism, 1909–1912," in the *Wisconsin Magazine of History*, 40:161–168 (Spring, 1957).

La Follette, Belle Case and Fola. *Robert M. La Follette* (2 vols., New York, 1953).

La Follette, Robert M. *La Follette's Autobiography* (Madison, reprint ed., 1960).

Margulies, Herbert F. "The Background of the La Follette-McGovern Schism," in the *Wisconsin Magazine of History*, 40:21–29 (Autumn, 1956).

————. "The Decline of Wisconsin Progressivism, 1911–1914," in *Mid-America*, 39:131–155 (July, 1957).

————. "The Election of 1920 in Wisconsin: The Return to 'Normalcy' Reappraised," in the *Wisconsin Magazine of History*, 41:15–22 (Autumn, 1957).

————. "Political Weaknesses in Wisconsin Progressivism, 1905–1908," in *Mid-America*, 41:154–172 (July, 1959).

Maxwell, Robert S. "La Follette and the Election of 1900: A Half Century Reappraisal," in the *Wisconsin Magazine of History*, 35:23–29, 68–71 (Autumn, 1951).

————. *Emanuel L. Philipp: Wisconsin Stalwart* (Madison, 1959).

————. *La Follette and the Rise of the Progressives in Wisconsin* (Madison, 1956).

McDonald, Forrest. *Let There Be Light: The Electric Utility Industry in Wisconsin, 1881–1955* (Madison, 1957).

Neu, Charles E. "Olympia Brown and the Woman's Suffrage Movement," in the *Wisconsin Magazine of History*, 43:277–287 (Summer, 1960).

Nye, Russell B. *Midwestern Progressive Politics* (East Lansing, Michigan, rev. ed., 1959).

Olson, Frederick I. "The Socialist Party and the Union in Milwaukee, 1900–1912," in the *Wisconsin Magazine of History*, 44:110–116 (Winter, 1960–1961).

Raney, William Francis. *Wisconsin: A Story of Progress* (New York, 1940), 282–359, 372–397.

Reinders, Robert C. "Daniel W. Hoan and the Milwaukee Socialist Party During the First World War," in the *Wisconsin Magazine of History*, 36:48–55 (Autumn, 1952).

Rosentreter, Frederick M. *The Boundaries of the Campus: A History of the University of Wisconsin Extension Division, 1885–1945* (Madison, 1957).

Saloutos, Theodore. "The Wisconsin Society of Equity," in *Agricultural History*, 14:78–95 (April, 1940).

————. "The Decline of the Wisconsin Society of Equity," in *Agricultural History*, 15:137–150 (July, 1941).

Saloutos, Theodore and Hicks, John D. *Agricultural Discontent in the Middle West, 1900–1939* (Madison, 1951).

Stephenson, Isaac. *Recollections of a Long Life, 1829–1915* (Chicago, 1916).

Still, Bayrd. *Milwaukee: The History of a City* (Madison, 1948), 431–497.

Vance, Maurice M. *Charles Richard Van Hise, Scientist Progressive* (Madison, 1961).

Wachman, Marvin. *History of the Social-Democratic Party of Milwaukee, 1897–1910* (Urbana, Ill., 1945).

Warren, Earl. "Robert M. La Follette, Sr.," in the *Wisconsin Magazine of History*, 38:195–198 (Summer, 1955).

Witte, Edwin E. "Labor in Wisconsin History," in the *Wisconsin Magazine of History*, 35:83–86, 137–142 (Winter, 1951).

————. "Statistics Relating to Wisconsin from the 1920 Census," in the *Wisconsin Blue Book, 1923*, 17–40.

Woerdehoff, Frank J. "Dr. Charles McCarthy: Planner of the Wisconsin System of Vocational and Adult Education," in the *Wisconsin Magazine of History*, 41:270–274 (Summer, 1958).

————. "Dr. Charles McCarthy's Role in Revitalizing the University Extension Division," in the *Wisconsin Magazine of History*, 40:13–18 (Autumn, 1956).

Work, John. "The First World War," in the *Wisconsin Magazine of History*, 41:32–44 (Autumn, 1957).

CHAPTER 7

Wisconsin in a Complex World
1925–1960

T HE years from 1925 to 1960 brought more diversity into
nearly all aspects of Wisconsin's history than had previously appeared. The state was compelled to make economic and political adjustments in order to participate
adequately in a world that was increasingly complex. The
simple moral formula of the older political Progressives
was no longer satisfactory, even for those who followed
the leadership of Robert La Follette, Jr., and his brother
Philip in their revival of Progressivism on a state and
national level. There was no single answer to the various
problems which arose, often from conditions and developments far outside Wisconsin's borders.

Foremost among the events affecting life in Wisconsin
were the great depression and two wars. All had world-
shaking consequences and all served to emphasize the in-

terdependent nature of twentieth century life in Wisconsin. Meeting the new conditions required resources beyond those found in the state, and one outcome of the effort was that Wisconsin citizens found themselves even more directly under the influence of the national government than they had been earlier.

At the same time that Wisconsin came to be more directly affected by developments on the national scene, it also contributed ideas, practices, and material to those developments. Several of the ingredients of Wisconsin progressive government as well as some of its personnel were borrowed by the government in Washington. In time of war food products from Wisconsin farms and dairy processors and a variety of essential manufactured products from Wisconsin's industries helped supply and arm the various military services. Wisconsin continued to enjoy a deserved reputation as a well-run state characterized by efficient government and honest administration.

Although by 1950 Wisconsin's lead as a dairy state went unchallenged, only 18.6 per cent of the population was engaged in agriculture. Of that percentage the great majority were dairy farmers. In 1957 Wisconsin's cattle population of 4,341,000 was substantially larger than the number of people in the state. Wisconsin's dairies used modern equipment and machinery, and their products were shipped by improved transportation methods and marketed according to the latest techniques of selling. In 1952 the dairy farmers began to ship their fluid milk in the large, bulk tank trucks that so quickly became a common sight on Wisconsin highways. Thirty-three Wisconsin creameries joined with nearly four hundred others from eight states in the co-operative marketing of their high-grade butter and other dairy products through the Land O'Lakes Creameries, Incorporated, which began its operations as an effective merchandising organization in 1924

A Wisconsin dairy farm—*El' Nathan M. Juedes Photo*
SHSW Colls.

In 1954 more than 64 per cent of Wisconsin's 35,000,-000 acres was in farms, and the average size farm was 146.6 acres. Besides dairying, Wisconsin farmers continued to raise tobacco, sugar beets, cranberries, fruit trees, potatoes, peas, and other vegetables. Many of these were raised near canneries where they were processed and, increasingly, migrant workers from the South, Mexico, or the British West Indies harvested them. In the summer of 1957, 16,000 migrant farm workers added to Wisconsin's farm labor supply.

Modernization and mechanization affected the lives of farm families as well as farm work. By 1954 the great majority of Wisconsin farmers owned passenger automobiles, and 66.9 per cent of the farm homes had telephones. Electricity with its benefits to the housewife and her farmer husband serviced 96.8 per cent of Wisconsin farms in 1954. Each of these improvements saved time and also brought the farmer and the members of his family into closer and more frequent contact with the people of the cities. In the specialized, technological world of the mid-twentieth century, farmers became still less the independent yeomen of an earlier day and still more, skilled workers in a complex and often unpredictable economy.

With each passing decade more Wisconsin communities classified as urban with a population of 2,500 or more, and in turn the number of people living and working in the larger industrial cities also grew. In 1960 more than half of the state's residents lived in urban communities; Milwaukee, with its population of 741,324, remained Wisconsin's leading metropolis and center of industrial life. Such Wisconsin cities as Madison, Superior, Kenosha, Racine, La Crosse and Eau Claire also contained important industries and played an increasingly important role in the economic and political development of the state.

Suburban housing development, Milwaukee
Milwaukee Journal Photo—SHSW Colls.

WISCONSIN'S LARGEST CITIES

The 1960 census revealed the following to be Wisconsin's ten largest cities:

City	Population
Milwaukee	741,324
Madison	126,706
Racine	89,144
West Allis	68,157
Kenosha	67,899
Green Bay	62,888
Wauwatosa	56,923
Appleton	48,411
La Crosse	47,575
Sheboygan	45,747

Even the physical appearance of Wisconsin's cities took on a changed look with the passing of the years. In Milwaukee, for instance, buses replaced the older electric streetcars. The older-style architecture of the business district provided striking contrast to the more modern, many-storied buildings on Wisconsin Avenue. The nationwide movement from the crowded cities to the suburbs also affected Milwaukee and made commuters out of many of the residents of the metropolitan area. More and more of those who visited the city for business or for pleasure arrived by air. In 1927 the first air passengers flew from Milwaukee to Chicago and the following year regular flights were scheduled from Milwaukee to Green Bay. By 1940 the bustling Milwaukee airport was one of America's leading civilian airports.

Milwaukee airport
Milwaukee Journal Photo—SHSW Colls.

Milwaukee was only one of a number of Wisconsin cities whose population growth and many industrial, commercial, educational, and political activities contributed to a more highly industrialized and diversified state. Madison also played a vital role in the transformation. Besides serving as state capital and Dane County seat, Madison, located in a rich agricultural and dairy region, became an important commercial center. By 1960 the population was 126,706, with thousands of its residents finding employment in Madison's numerous federal, state, county, and city offices. Others worked in such a variety of occupations as food processing and the manufacturing of machine tools, dry cell batteries, chemical fertilizers, hospital equipment, and farm machinery.

As a cultural center, Madison also contributed greatly to the state and the nation. In 1961 more than 19,000 students attended the University which had played so significant a part in the state's history. Many other thousands visited the city to enjoy its parks, its fine lake shore drive, or to use the resources of the State Historical Society or one of the other libraries in Madison. Some students and visitors came from distant parts of the world. The cosmopolitan blend of peoples in Madison continued to contain a majority element of older Wisconsin stock, many of whose grandparents had also come to the Badger State from Germany or the Scandinavian countries.

In the northwestern section of Wisconsin, Superior became an important commercial city which in 1960 had a population of 33,058. Located on Lake Superior, the city built an excellent harbor which connected with a number of railroads. Great quantities of iron ore and grain left Superior to be shipped eastward across the lakes, while returning barges were often piled high with coal for distribution in the area. Some was used in the city's nu-

Loading ore at Superior
SHSW Colls.

merous iron and steel mills. The city also had shipyards as well as the flour and planing mills which used some of the lumber and grain produced in the surrounding region.

Kenosha and Racine, both located on Lake Michigan, also combined commerce and industry. In 1960 Kenosha had a population of 67,899 and Racine, 89,144. Leading Kenosha industrial products included metal goods, fire engines, mattresses, tools, underwear and wire rope, while Racine's plants and factories turned out farm machinery, floor wax, malted milk, luggage, furniture, hardware, and electrical equipment. In the nineteenth century the fine Racine harbor specialized in shipping grain, later shifting to industrial products.

Eau Claire in the northwest and La Crosse on the Mississippi were two other industrial and commercial Wisconsin cities. Eau Claire, located at the mouth of the Eau Claire River and at the head of the navigable part of the Chippewa served as the commercial center for northwestern Wisconsin and the outlet for the Chippewa lumber district. Among its manufactured products were tires, pressure cookers, aluminum ware, and refrigerators. La Crosse was the trade center for a fine dairy region and earlier specialized in manufacturing wooden products. In later years La Crosse became noted for such products as automobile instruments and farm machinery. Its population in 1960 was 47,575.

Wisconsin's cities nearly all specialized in some products vital to the complex life of mid-twentieth century America. In 1955, 463,965 people in the state were employed in some kind of manufacturing establishment. The major industry was the production of non-electrical machinery such as the huge papermaking machines that were made in Beloit, and steam shovels and other excavating equipment. The processing of food and related products was Wisconsin's second most important industry in terms of numbers employed; the manufacture of electrical machinery was third. The state also ranked high in the production of small gasoline engines, outboard motors, diesel engines, paper, automobiles and trucks, farm machinery, and enameled ware. Wisconsin industry became as diversified as its agriculture and like farming it, too, found it necessary to adjust to new conditions and needs.

Commercial changes followed naturally in the wake of other economic changes in Wisconsin and the rest of the country. The advertising and selling of goods provided work for a large percentage of the state's employed population. In 1954, more than 45,000 people working in Wisconsin were engaged in the wholesale trade and the state's 47,884 retail trade establishments employed still another 164,030 people. Each year, as more flour came in from Minnesota's Twin Cities, the Milwaukee traffic in grain declined and other items loomed larger in the lake port's trade. Wool and meat from the West, steel from Illinois, and coal from Pennsylvania arrived in steadily increasing amounts. In 1936 tankers began to carry oil across the lakes from the East. Packaged foods and manufactured articles came to Milwaukee from all sections of the United States and the world. Railroads declined in importance with the increased use of airplanes and motor trucks in the commercial carrying trade. But the latest major change affecting Wisconsin commerce was really an updating of the oldest kind of transportation. In 1959 the opening of the St. Lawrence Seaway made Milwaukee an ocean port and promised an even more expanded commercial life to the city, despite its continuing and uphill battle with Chicago to the south, another terminus of the newly-created seaway.

By the second decade of the twentieth century, Wis-

Reforestation means trees for tomorrow
SHSW Colls.—Frank A. Ross Studio

consin officials had come to realize that not all of Wisconsin land was good for either agriculture or industry. Two laws provided a working basis for intelligent use of much of the land in the sparsely settled northern counties. A multitude of farm failures and a high percentage of tax delinquency convinced even some of those who had promoted farm settlement in the cutover lands that the land might be put to better use as forest land. The forest crop law of 1927 enabled landholders to enter contractual agreements with the state for growing timber. The contracts were to run for as long as fifty years. The proprietor paid a nominal annual tax of 10 cents an acre until the trees were cut, at which time he was to pay a severance tax of 10 per cent of the value of the crop. Because of the special rate of taxation provided in the law it was necessary first to ratify a constitutional amendment permitting the procedure. Another law of 1927 authorized Wisconsin counties to establish county forests. These were followed by legislation in 1929 which allowed counties to zone their rural lands for agriculture, forestry, or recreation. By 1957, 27 Wisconsin counties had established forests with a total of 2,178,826 acres. More than 5,000,000 acres had been set aside for either forestry or recreation, thus ending the problem of trying to farm so much of the cutover land that had proved to be unsuited for agriculture.

The new policy also helped develop Wisconsin's growing tourist trade. The state's eight thousand lakes and numerous rivers stocked with fish, its hunting areas, and scenic spots attract thousands of visitors each year. After 1935 Wisconsin provided money for advertising its northern vacation spots. A state conservation department publicized the state as a recreation area and managed the state forests, regulated hunting and fishing, fought forest fires, and educated people to prevent them, and carried on other activities relating to the protection and preservation of Wisconsin's outdoor resources. One estimate placed the value of Wisconsin's tourist industry as high as half a billion dollars annually.

While Wisconsin residents made excellent use of their economic resources and political leadership during the first half of the twentieth century, they also gave attention to a variety of cultural activities. Outstanding scholars, attracted by the excellent library facilities and atmosphere of academic freedom, continued to enhance the reputation of the University of Wisconsin as a world-re-

Boating on one of Wisconsin's lakes
Milwaukee Journal Photo—SHSW Colls.

nowned center of research and teaching. In the early 1920's, the University began extending its educational and cultural advantages to the people of the state through the services of its radio station WHA. From experimental broadcasting in 1917, the facilities were extended until the station broadcasted over a hundred hours a week, offering a wide variety of farm, homemaking, and general cultural and intellectual programs as well as regular news and weather reports. In later years the University added educational television broadcasts.

The other state colleges and the public schools also underwent a number of significant changes. An increasing number of young people attended school for a longer period of time and most of them were taught by teachers who had more formal training than those of earlier times. By the middle of the 1950's most Wisconsin secondary school teachers had gone to college for at least four years, though many elementary teachers had received only half as much training beyond high school. The law requires Wisconsin children to attend some kind of vocational or academic secondary school full-time until the age of 16 or until they graduate from high school. The cost of Wisconsin's entire system of public education soared from $82,335,821 for the 1944–45 school year to $377,018,089 for 1957–58.

In the area of state-supported higher education the University established a number of extension centers in various cities. In 1911 some of the state normal schools began to offer two years of college work, and in 1925 the legislature authorized them to grant a Bachelor of Education degree. Two years later the normal schools became four-year teachers colleges and in 1951 another change made them simply state colleges with authority to grant liberal arts degrees as well as degrees in education. In 1955 a thoroughgoing reorganization of the state's system of higher education included combining Milwaukee's state college and extension center as part of the University and establishing a co-ordinating committee consisting of members of the Boards of Regents of the University and the state colleges. The new committee received considerable power over finances, property, and the programs of the institutions involved in order to plan effectively for anticipated increases in enrollments.

During the first half of the twentieth century, Wisconsin also made some contributions to the drama and visual arts. In 1909 Mrs. Laura Sherry of Milwaukee founded the Wisconsin Players, a community project that led to the beginning of the little theatre movement which quickly spread across the nation. In 1940 the Farm and Home Week at Madison included an exhibit of various sculptoring, wood carving, and painting done by farm men and women which revealed a considerable amount of unsuspected talent and started the practice of having such an exhibition annually. There were also professional artists working in Wisconsin, though only a few attained an outstanding national reputation such as those enjoyed by John Stewart Curry, who was a resident artist at the University from 1936 to 1946, and Aaron Bohrod, who served in the same capacity after Curry's death.

Wisconsin writers also brought attention to the Badger State, although a number of them wrote about the Wisconsin scene after moving elsewhere. John Muir, the famous naturalist and conservationist, commented on his Wisconsin days as a child, young man and university student in his autobiographical *The Story of My Boyhood and Youth* which was published in 1912. Edna Ferber drew heavily upon her early Wisconsin experiences for the settings of a number of her novels including *Fanny Herself* and her 1935 novel of the lumber barons, *Come and Get It*. One of Wisconsin's best known writers, West

Salem-born Hamlin Garland, lived in the state only nine years, but he maintained numerous contacts with writers and friends in his home state. In his early fiction Garland used Wisconsin material, and one of his early novels, *Rose of Dutcher's Coolly,* he considered his "one Wisconsin novel." His pioneer writings in the realistic school of fiction dealt mostly with the harsher aspects of farm life in the Middle West. In 1926 the state University granted an honorary degree to Garland, citing him as "a son of Wisconsin who has gained the admiration of the country as the preserver of the fact and flavor that gave identity to the Middle Border from which we spring."

Some of Wisconsin's better-known literary figures spent their most productive years in the state. Zona Gale wrote numerous plays, short stories, and novels in her Portage home. Beginning as a sentimental writer she later pictured some of the less pleasant aspects of life according to

Zona Gale
SHSW Colls.

the "realistic" literary school of the time. Her play, *Miss Lulu Bett,* received a Pulitzer Prize in 1921 and gave its author national recognition. Zona Gale was also an ardent promoter of the little theatre movement, a strong political Progressive and a member of the University Board of Regents. William Ellery Leonard, a member of the University's English department from 1906 until his death in 1944, gained distinction as a writer of prose and poetry. During World War I Leonard continued to support La Follette and gave vent to his feelings in several poetic protests, including "The Lynching Bee," and "The Old Agitator," a word portrait of the anti-war Socialist, Eugene V. Debs. His *Two Lives* became a best seller in 1925 and two years later an autobiography, *The Locomotive-God,* appeared. August Derleth of Sauk City, writing novels, biography, poetry, and regional history, won clear

Frank Lloyd Wright
SHSW Colls.

title to being Wisconsin's most prolific author. Derleth's most ambitious literary project consists of a proposed multi-volume *Sac Prairie Saga* which is to portray a century of life in the region where he was born and has made his home. Among his better-known writings were *The Wisconsin: River of a Thousand Isles* for the "Rivers of America" series, and *Still Small Voice: The Biography of Zona Gale.*

No other Wisconsin cultural figure achieved greater world-wide recognition or exerted more influence than the architect Frank Lloyd Wright, who was born at Richland Center in 1869. Wright studied engineering at the University but left to work in Chicago before completing the course. From 1888 to 1896 he worked as a draftsman in the firm of Adler and Sullivan and he then opened his own office. His employer, Louis Sullivan, had pioneered with early functional architecture and maintained that a building's form should grow out of the function for which it was designed. Sullivan's ideas and work profoundly influenced the young Wright, who later referred to Sullivan as *Lieber Meister*. Wright's early buildings were conventional and traditional, but he soon surpassed Sullivan's earlier experimental ventures and began a career which eventually made him the world's best-known architect.

Wright believed that architecture should be organically related to its environment, and that the machine enabled builders to create new forms by using newly-devised materials. In the early twentieth century he designed low-lying prairie houses which employed the horizontal line of the Illinois landscape. He used even more daring innovations in such creations as the Hollyhock House in California, the Unity Temple in Oak Park, Illinois, the S. C. Johnson office building in Racine, and the Larkin Building in Buffalo. During World War I, Wright supervised the building of Japan's Imperial Hotel in Tokyo, which he designed sufficiently flexible to withstand the serious earthquake of 1923 unscathed. In later years he designed the Unitarian Meetinghouse in Madison, completed in 1951, and the Guggenheim Art Museum in New York. Among Wright's many other plans for buildings were a mile-high skyscraper in Chicago, an opera house in Baghdad, and a civic center for Madison's Monona lake front. By the time of his death in early 1959 Wright had designed more than six hundred buildings.

No other American architect had so profoundly influenced the art as did Frank Lloyd Wright. Apprentices from all over the world studied under him at his school for architecture, Taliesen, which had a summer location near Spring Green, Wisconsin, and a winter location in Taliesen West at Scottsdale, Arizona. Wright explained

Unitarian   Meetinghouse,
Madison
William Wollin—SHSW Colls.

In his 1932 autobiography Frank Lloyd Wright put down some of his ideas about the relationship between architecture and its natural environment. The following passage concerns the first Taliesin, built at Spring Green in 1911:

I wished to be part of my beloved southern Wisconsin and not put my small part of it out of countenance. Architecture, after all, I have learned, or before all, I should say, is no less a weaving and a fabric than the trees. And as anyone might see, a beech tree is a beech tree. It isn't trying to be an oak. Nor is a pine trying to be a birch although each makes the other more beautiful when seen together.

The world has had appropriate buildings before—why not more appropriate buildings now than ever before? There must be some kind of house that would belong to that hill, as trees and the ledges of rock did; as Grandfather and Mother had belonged to it, in their sense of it all.

Yes, there must be a natural house, not natural as caves and log-cabins were natural but native in spirit and making, with all that architecture had meant whenever it was alive in times past. Nothing at all that I had ever seen would do. This country had changed all that into something else. Grandfather and Grandmother were something splendid in themselves that I couldn't imagine in period houses I had ever seen. But there was a house that hill might marry and live happily with ever after. I fully intended to find it. I even saw, for myself, what it might be like and began to build it as the "brow" of the hill.—Edgar Kaufman and Ben Raeburn, eds., *Frank Lloyd Wright: Writings and Buildings* (New York, 1960), 174.

his concept of architecture in a number of books including an unusually frank and complete *Autobiography*. Several European editions of his work spread his fame abroad and made him a leading figure in a modern architecture movement. Actually, Wright belonged to no school of architecture; he was always an individualist and expressed his unique personality in his life and in his work. "Individuality is the most precious thing in life . . . ," said Wright in his autobiography, and his masterpieces of architecture are proof of his faith.

During some of the years when Frank Lloyd Wright exerted his individualism in architecture, many Americans

SHSW Colls.

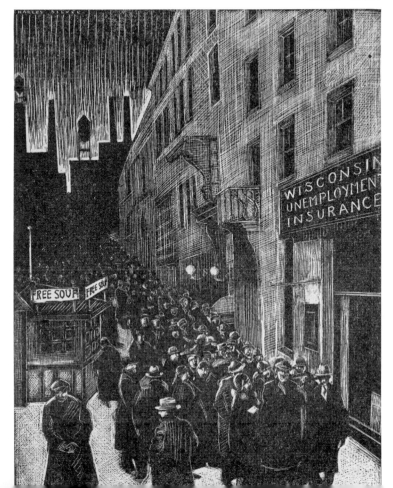

had their faith in economic individualism rudely shaken by the nation's most severe and prolonged depression. The boom prosperity of the twenties came to a sudden halt with the stock market crash of October, 1929, and what at first appeared to be a slight recession soon proved much more serious. Wisconsin industry suffered severely, factories closed down, wages dropped, and the unemployment lists swelled. By 1929, despite a trend towards consolidation in banking, the state still had too many small banks. Many of the weaker ones failed and in March, 1933, the newly-elected Democratic governor, Albert George Schmedeman, declared a two-week statewide banking moratorium. The collapse of Wisconsin's banking system was unparalleled in the state's history and recovery proved to be a slow, painful process.

The depression hit especially hard in Milwaukee which had earlier prospered so well with its diversified industrial life. By 1933 there was a 75 per cent decline from the number of people who had been employed in Milwaukee in 1929, and that year the city collected less than half of the assessed property taxes. In April of 1933 approximately 140,000 people in Milwaukee, or one in five of the population, received some form of direct relief, which was then supplied by the county. Mayor Daniel W. Hoan helped organize a United States Conference of Mayors, which in 1933 pressured Washington for national relief. The federal government responded with $300,000,000 for direct relief to stricken cities, and later with a multitude of relief and public works measures. Under the Public Works Administration Milwaukee gained employment for many of its people and got new streets, sewers, city parks, playgrounds and a plant for purifying water.

One of the results of the great depression was the national electorate's accepting the leadership of Franklin D. Roosevelt and his Democratic program for recovery, the

New Deal. Wisconsin made some substantial contributions to the New Deal itself. The Wisconsin Idea, with its
emphasis on the use of experts in public administration,

---

was clearly a precedent for President Roosevelt's "brain
trust." Wisconsin's pioneer old age pension law of 1925
and unemployment compensation law of 1931 were both
models for the federal Social Security Act of 1935, which
was based on recommendations made by Wisconsin economist Edwin E. Witte, executive director of the technical
board studying the problem of economic security. The
national administration also used the talent and experience of Arthur J. Altmeyer, who was secretary of the Wis-

consin Industrial Commission when he became President Roosevelt's Assistant Secretary of Labor. Several leading New Deal bureaucrats had had earlier government careers in Wisconsin, including Leo T. Crowley of Milton Junction, who had served as Governor Schmedeman's secretary and adviser before he went to Washington to hold a number of important jobs, and David Lilienthal, who had been the head of Wisconsin's Public Service Commission under Governor La Follette and then headed the Tennessee Valley Authority, and still later the Atomic Energy Commission. Historians have debated the relation of Progressivism to the New Deal; certainly the Wisconsin contributions were just a few of many influences on the Roosevelt program, yet in some instances New Deal practices were clearly rooted in Wisconsin experiences. Whether the national use of the Wisconsin ideas contributed to the creation of a national movement in the spirit of Progressivism or to the erection of a huge, impersonal bureaucracy, far removed from the control of the electorate, remained a subject for scholarly and political argument.

The various New Deal measures taken to cope with the depression all gave some relief to the state and many of them also brought more lasting benefits. Various work programs gave people employment building roads, widening streets, and constructing post offices and other public buildings. The W.P.A. program offered jobs to thousands and used skills ranging from pick and shovel manual labor to those of highly trained scholars, artists, and writers. By the time it was terminated in 1943, the W.P.A. had brought $369,000,000 into Wisconsin. Inevitably, however, each of the New Deal measures made the states more dependent upon the national government. They had to comply with a great number of federal rules and regulations in order to receive the various benefits provided by C.W.A.,

P.W.A., W.P.A., and relief grants from the Reconstruction Finance Corporation and other New Deal agencies.

Even before the New Deal, Wisconsin began its attack on the depression under the leadership of Governor Philip La Follette. Early in the depression La Follette urged that a public works program should provide employment at state expense constructing highway overpasses and underpasses at dangerous railroad crossings. The money came from a higher gasoline tax. Between 1931 and 1933 eighty bypasses were constructed at a cost of $7,000,000. In 1932 Wisconsin set a precedent when the legislature passed the first state unemployment insurance act, later copied by other states as well as the national government. La Follette also used experts in advising his administration and successfully promoted a labor code which favored unions and checked the use of injunctions in labor disputes.

Hydroelectric dam on the Wisconsin River, Sauk City

In his second and third administrations (1935–1939), Governor La Follette promoted a program of social and economic legislation that came to be known as Wisconsin's "Little New Deal." The state had its own N.R.A. which permitted the governor to establish codes of fair labor practice, a variety of T.V.A. in the Wisconsin Development Authority which promoted cheaper power, heat, and light, its own version of A.A.A. in the Wisconsin Agricultural Authority designed to aid the farmer to market his products co-operatively and to obtain better prices for his crops, its own Wagner Act with a state law establishing a labor relations board to settle labor disputes. Governor La Follette's "Little New Deal" failed to win the same intensity of approval that voters apparently gave to the program of President Franklin D. Roosevelt, for Republican Governor Julius P. Heil, who won the election of 1938, successfully demolished most of the La Follette program by cutting off funds and abolishing or radically modifying the newly-created state agencies one by one.

Not all of the New Deal or the Wisconsin program to meet the depression crisis were aimed at the urban unemployed. For America's farmers, the depression began shortly after the close of World War I. From then on they found that the mounting cost of farm needs and farm machinery could not be met by a corresponding rise in the prices they obtained for their products. More often than not, farm land decreased instead of increased in value. A growing percentage of farmers rented the land they worked and many of those who owned their farms found it necessary to mortgage them. Many lost their farms by foreclosure on mortgages they had optimistically taken on the property. Commercial farming was closely tied to international conditions and to the national economy, and the depression hit the farmer after he had already suffered economic setbacks for a decade. Not all of Wisconsin's farmers suffered to the same extent, however. At least those who raised the bulk of their own food had something to eat. There was also inequality among the dairy farmers. Those who sold their milk to creameries and cheese factories received as little as $0.75 or $0.80 per hundred pounds, while those who sent fluid milk to city consumers fared much better, getting $1.50 for the same amount.

Farm foreclosures, mounting debts, desperation brought on by hunger and the agitation of a few dairy farm leaders set off a series of Wisconsin milk strikes in 1933. The Farm Holiday, a national farm association, and the Wisconsin Co-operative Milk Pool spearheaded the action, although in two of the three Wisconsin strikes the Pool had to carry on alone. The aim of the strike was to force the price of milk up to a minimum of $1.40 per hundred pounds, but only a fraction of the state's dairy farmers participated. A fortunate 10 per cent got higher prices

Milk strike, 1934

for fluid milk, and many others preferred the lower prices to no cash income at all. The striking farmers blocked roadways, dumped milk and, on occasion, planted bombs in cheese factories. National guardsmen clashed with the pickets and used tear and emetic gas to disperse them. Three persons were killed in the strikes which gradually died out by early November, 1933, after dramatizing their plight to the nation, but without getting higher prices.

Wisconsin farmers got relief in other ways. A series of mortgage moratorium laws gave farmers a longer period of time to redeem their property and encouraged creditors to scale down their debts. The national Farm Credit Association and the Wisconsin Farm and Credit Association both acted to keep farm foreclosures to a minimum. Other federal funds went to farmers to purchase seed grain and livestock feed under the guise of drought relief. The Rural Electrification Administration lent money to co-operative associations created to extend electrical service to rural patrons. The Agricultural Adjustment Administration contracted farmers to pay them for not growing crops in an effort to raise prices by curtailing farm production. When the Supreme Court threw out the A.A.A. much the same program continued as part of a new Soil Conservation and Domestic Allotment Act. In Wisconsin, growers of sugar beets, tobacco, wheat, and feed corn benefitted from these programs. As early as 1931 dairy farmers received a token gesture of state aid when the legislature imposed a $0.06 per pound tax on oleomargarine. When this proved insufficient to stop the use of margarine the tax was raised to $0.15 in 1935, although its actual effect as a kind of protective tariff in the interest of dairy farmers and the butter creameries is not determinable. Probably Wisconsin citizens' preference for the product of its dairy farms acted as a greater influence than the tax. Government relief programs and subsidies also helped the farmers, but prosperity in both the agricultural and industrial areas did not return until the defense program of World War II got underway. It was the war itself that finally ended the depression.

Politically, Wisconsin continued the era of efficient administration and graft-free government which had been so vital a part of the Progressive movement. However, a second phase of Progressivism under the leadership of Robert La Follette, Jr., "Young Bob," and his brother Phil lacked the fire and enthusiasm of the earlier crusade and eventually died out. When the elder La Follette died his son Bob succeeded in winning the nomination and election to his unfilled term in the United States Senate, a position he held for twenty-one years. In the Senate La Follette proved himself to be just as independently progressive as his father had been. Although he was quiet and studious rather than a fiery orator, young La Follette gained national attention for a number of his acts. He helped defeat a third term for stalwart Republican President Calvin Coolidge, instigated and led a government civil liberties investigation which revealed the widespread use of labor spies in American industry, dramatically called attention to the difficult plight of the drought-stricken farmers of the Midwest, and headed a joint House-Senate committee whose findings led to the Congressional Reorganization Act of 1946 making Congressional procedure more efficient. La Follette supported most of President Franklin D. Roosevelt's domestic New Deal program but he clashed with him on matters of foreign policy.

Like his father, young Bob believed that it was in the best interest of the nation to avoid international commitments which might lead to involvement in foreign wars.

His first speech in the Senate was in opposition to America's joining the World Court. He also feared that too much emphasis on defense and mobilization would give certain vested business interests an opportunity to limit the rights of labor. "We must put our social, economic and spiritual house in order," said La Follette in 1940, "if democracy is to survive in the New World." Specifically, he opposed peacetime conscription, modification of neutrality legislation, granting the President the power to take over a defense plant during a strike or threat of a strike, and the lend-lease and other Roosevelt policies which he felt would lead America step by step into World War II.

Although he remained consistently anti-war, Young Bob was neither a pacifist nor an isolationist. "I am not an isolationist," said La Follette, "except in the sense of the President's speech at Chautauqua in 1936 when he said: 'We are not isolationists except in so far as we seek to isolate ourselves completely from war.'" Political opponents used the term "Isolationist" loosely to discredit La Follette and others who opposed the administration's pro-Allied foreign policy, but Young Bob's position on a number of foreign relations issues made the term meaningless when applied to him. Although he basically agreed with some of his father's ideas, he also realized that the oversimplified concepts of an earlier time could only handicap his own political career. La Follette supported Secretary of State Cordell Hull's reciprocal trade program and also his "Good Neighbor" policy in Latin America, and he later endorsed the idea of the United Nations. When the United States entered the war La Follette supported it. In June, 1944, for his contributions to thinking about foreign policy, *Life* magazine characterized La Follette as "the conscience of America." In 1946 La Follette failed to win re-nomination in the Wisconsin primary. The victor was Joseph R. McCarthy of Appleton.

During most of his public life young Bob La Follette, like his father, worked within the ranks of the Republican Party. His brother Philip, who also started his political career as a Republican, was elected district attorney for Dane County in 1924 and became governor in 1930. Two previous governors, Fred R. Zimmerman and Walter J. Kohler, had both served only one term each, and at the end of his two-year term Governor La Follette, too, lost his bid for re-election. It was 1932, and the national Democratic landslide of that year brought Albert G. Schemedeman into the state executive office. Schmedeman, the first Democratic governor in Wisconsin since George W. Peck filled the office from 1891 to 1895, served only one term before Phil La Follette resumed the post, this time as a representative of the new Progressive Party.

In 1934 the La Follettes and a number of other Progressives, including William T. Evjue, then editor of La Follette's *Progressive* magazine and of Madison's *Capital Times,* decided that the time was ripe for the formation of a new third party in Wisconsin. They charged that both of the old parties were bound by tradition and too deeply committed to private vested interests to support a truly progressive program. Probably more practical political considerations also contributed to the decision. Both Robert La Follette, Jr. and Philip were up for re-election as senator and governor and the Republican Party was temporarily discredited throughout the nation. On the other hand, the La Follettes saw little future for themselves in the state's Democratic organization. Therefore they organized a separate Progressive Party and called for an improved conservation program, the distribution of milk as a public utility, the initiative and referendum on the national level, and a popular referendum before any war could be declared.

The new party enjoyed the support of such Progressive

leaders as Gerald P. Nye of North Dakota, Montana's Burton K. Wheeler, and Fiorello La Guardia of New York. Both brothers ran for office under the slogan "Run with the La Follettes and win," and when the votes were counted the new party had proved itself a strong force. Phil was governor, Bob, Jr., senator, and the Progressives controlled the Wisconsin legislature and sent seven men to Congress. But the initial enthusiasm for revived Progressivism did not last. Governor La Follette's "Little New Deal" did not give sufficient benefits to the farmers to win their support, his reorganization of the state administrative machinery seemed to some to give him too much arbitrary power, and when the Progressive Board of Regents of the University dismissed President Glenn Frank, his friends proclaimed him a victim of La Follettism.

A National Progressive Party, launched by Phil La Follette in a mass meeting at the University's stock pavilion in April, 1938, proved a complete failure. A coalition of Democrats and Republicans placed Julius P. Heil, a Republican, in the governor's post and ousted La Follette. Opponents accused the La Follettes of attempting to organize a variety of American fascism, using the ridiculous charge that the new party's symbol, a voter's X in a circle, resembled the Nazi swastika. High taxes and a new business recession led voters throughout the North to turn again to the Republican Party. The unwillingness of progressive Democrats to support any move which might weaken their own party also contributed to the Progressive defeat. Later, Governor Heil's absenteeism from the Capitol, extravagant habits, and public clowning led to another reaction which enabled Wisconsin Progressives to elect Orland S. Loomis as a Republican candidate in 1942. Loomis died before taking office, however, and the lieutenant-governor, Walter S. Goodland, proved himself an honest and competent Republican governor.

Launching the National Progressive Party—*World Wide Photos*
SHSW Colls.

In 1946 Robert La Follette, Jr. disbanded the Progressive Party, led its followers back into the Republican Party, and tried without success to win the primary election and keep the seat in the Senate which he had held since his father's death in 1925. The demise of the Progressive Party and his defeat in the primaries signalled the end of the La Follette influence in Wisconsin politics. Young Bob moved to Washington where he acted as a legal adviser, legislative consultant, and lobbyist. After suffering several heart attacks, he took his own life in February, 1953, at the age of fifty-eight. Philip served on General MacArthur's staff in the Pacific during World War II and he later held a business post in Bayside, New York, before returning to practice law in Madison. For more than half a century the La Follettes had worked for their version of progressive reform in politics and their efforts often focused the national spotlight on themselves and on their native state. No other family had made a deeper impression on the political life of Wisconsin.

TERMS OF WISCONSIN'S GOVERNORS, 1927–1960

January, 1927–1929	Fred R. Zimmerman (Republican)
January, 1929–1931	Walter J. Kohler (Republican)
January, 1931–1933	Philip F. La Follette (Republican)
January, 1933–1935	Albert G. Schmedeman (Democrat)
January, 1935–1939	Philip F. La Follette (Progressive)
January, 1939–1943	Julius P. Heil (Republican) Orland Loomis (Progressive) *
January, 1943–1947	Walter S. Goodland (Republican)
March, 1947–1951	Oscar Rennebohm (Republican)
January, 1951–1957	Walter J. Kohler, Jr. (Republican)
January, 1957–1959	Vernon W. Thompson (Republican)
January, 1959–	Gaylord Nelson (Democrat)

—1958 *Blue Book* (Madison, 1958), p. 550

* Governor-elect Loomis died December 7, 1942, before his inauguration and Lieutenant-Governor Walter S. Goodland "was designated 'Acting Governor' for period of vacancy."

The La Follette's ill-fated attempt to found a National Progressive Party occurred just about a year before the outbreak of World War II in Europe. The war touched off a heated debate concerning the wisdom of President Roosevelt's various steps short of war in support of the Allied powers, a debate which came to a sudden halt on December 7, 1941, when the Japanese attacked Pearl Harbor. As did World War I, the Second World War ushered in a period of lush prosperity when domestic reform issues took a back seat to defense spending and military preparation. Both Wisconsin industry and agriculture shared the war prosperity. About two hundred firms in Milwaukee, Racine, Kenosha, Janesville, Beloit, and other Wisconsin communities had received defense contracts before Pearl Harbor put America into the war itself. Instead of the

Landing craft built in Wisconsin during World War II
SHSW Colls.

dreary unemployment which characterized the depression years, labor was in demand, and wages and prices **rose** steadily. Manitowoc, Sturgeon Bay, and Superior became large shipbuilding centers, turning out submarines and other types of marine craft. Shipbuilding proved to be Wisconsin's largest single item in the great number of special war orders. Farm produce also brought good prices and farmers, who a few years earlier had curtailed production, now furnished large quantities of dairy products, vegetables, poultry, and eggs for the armed services and the civilian population in the cities.

The state was geared to war and the state's government and population were more dependent upon orders from Washington than ever before. Anti-war sentiment virtually ended with America's entry into the conflict; there was neither the crusading enthusiasm nor the strong opposition minority which had been a part of Wisconsin's history in World War I. In October of 1940, Governor Julius P. Heil set up a twelve-member state council of defense to co-ordinate the federal, state, and local defense programs. Many Wisconsin men received their basic training at Camp McCoy near Sparta, or at Camp Williams. Madison's modern airport, renamed Truax Field, was an important center for training in the vital area of radio communication. The University and colleges introduced military training for their students and shared their facilities with special programs of the various armed services. Wisconsin's pioneer leadership in the area of extension education helped locate the United States Armed Forces Institute in Madison. The Institute (USAFI), in co-operation with the University, offered college-level correspondence courses in numerous subjects to American fighting men throughout the world.

The state's entire National Guard became a part of the nation's fighting machine, forming a substantial part of

Wisconsin War Heroes

top left:
Fleet Admiral William D. Leahy

top right:
General of the Army Douglas MacArthur

bottom:
Richard I. Bong
SHSW Colls.—U. S. Army and Navy Photos

the new Red Arrow or 32nd Division, just as it had in the earlier global conflict. The Red Arrow maintained the reputation of its predecessor and remained undefeated after a series of hard-fought campaigns against the Japanese in the southwest Pacific. Wisconsin shared its Red Arrow war record with men from Michigan and other states; the majority of the state's fighting men were draftees who served in units composed of men from all sections of the nation. Few of them received the notice that fell on Wisconsin-reared General Douglas MacArthur, Fleet Admiral William D. Leahy, or war ace Richard I. Bong of Poplar, who downed forty planes and received every decoration awarded to fliers, including the Congressional Medal of Honor. In November, 1944, about eight months before the war ended, an unofficial estimate placed Wisconsin's World War II death loss at 4,068.

After the Second World War foreign affairs played an increasingly important part in the lives of Wisconsin's citizens. People in the state were divided on such issues as the formation of the United Nations, American support for European recovery, and the growing power of the Soviet Union. But when the limited Korean War broke out in June, 1950, there was very little difference of opinion. Once again war brought an economic uplift to Wisconsin and the rest of the nation.

WISCONSIN'S PRESIDENTIAL VOTES, 1928–1960

1928	Herbert Hoover (Republican)	544,205
	Alfred E. Smith (Democrat)	450,259
	Norman Thomas (Socialist)	18,213
	William F. Varney (Prohibition)	2,245
	William Z. Foster (Workers)	1,528
	Verne L. Reynolds (Socialist Labor)	381

1932	Franklin D. Roosevelt (Democrat)	707,410
	Herbert Hoover (Republican)	347,741
	Norman Thomas (Socialist)	53,379
	William Z. Foster (Communist)	3,112
	William D. Upshaw (Prohibition)	2,672
	Verne L. Reynolds (Socialist Labor)	494
1936	Franklin D. Roosevelt (Democrat)	802,894
	Alfred M. Landon (Republican)	380,828
	William Lemke (Union)	60,297
	Norman Thomas (Socialist)	10,626
	Earl Browder (Communist)	2,197
	David L. Colvin (Prohibition)	1,071
	John W. Aiken (Socialist Labor)	557
1940	Franklin D. Roosevelt (Democrat)	704,821
	Wendell Willkie (Republican)	679,206
	Norman Thomas (Socialist)	15,071
	Earl Browder (Communist)	2,394
	Roger Babson (Prohibition)	2,148
	John W. Aiken (Socialist Labor)	1,882
1944	Thomas Dewey (Republican)	674,532
	Franklin D. Roosevelt (Democrat)	650,413
	Norman Thomas (Socialist)	13,205
	Edward Teichert (Independent)	1,002
1948	Harry S. Truman (Democrat)	647,310
	Thomas Dewey (Republican)	590,959
	Henry Wallace (People's Progressive)	25,282
	Norman Thomas (Socialist)	12,547
	Edward Teichert (Independent)	399
	Farrell Dobbs (Ind.-Socialist Workers)	303
1952	Dwight D. Eisenhower (Republican)	979,744
	Adlai E. Stevenson (Democrat)	622,175
	Vincent Hallinan (Ind.-Progressive)	2,174

	Farrell Dobbs (Ind.-Socialist Workers)	1,350
	Darlington Hoopes (Ind.-Socialist)	1,157
	Eric Hass (Independent-Socialist Labor)	770
1956	Dwight D. Eisenhower (Republican)	954,854
	Adlai E. Stevenson (Democrat)	586,768
	T. Coleman Andrews (Independent)	6,918
	Darlington Hoopes (Independent)	754
	Eric Hass (Independent)	710
	Farrell Dobbs (Independent)	564
1960	Richard M. Nixon (Republican)	895,175
	John F. Kennedy (Democrat)	830,805
	Farrell Dobbs (Socialist Worker)	1,792
	Eric Hass (Socialist Labor)	1,310

It was the postwar setting of the cold war which gave importance to Wisconsin's Senator Joseph R. McCarthy, who defeated Robert La Follette, Jr. in the 1946 Republican primary and won his seat in the Senate. McCarthy began his political career as a Democrat in 1936 when he ran for district attorney of Shawano County and polled 577 votes to his victorious Progressive opponent's 3,014. He later became a Republican and in 1939 won election as a state circuit judge. McCarthy's first few years in the Senate were uneventful, but he quickly entered the headlines in 1950 after a speech in Wheeling, West Virginia, in which he claimed to have the names of Communists employed in the State Department. His single-minded crusade against Communists in the government made Senator McCarthy one of the most controversial personalities in recent history. Although to many people outside the state, McCarthy's name automatically brought Wisconsin to mind, he was mostly concerned with national rather than state issues. By the time of his death in 1957, during his second term as senator, he was no longer a headline figure.

Governor Walter J. Kohler, Jr., became the Republican candidate for Senator McCarthy's unexpired term, but he lost to William Proxmire, his Democratic opponent. Proxmire's election was symbolic of a change which had been developing in Wisconsin politics and which reflected in part the growing political significance of its city population. It was a major Democratic victory but not an isolated phenomenon. In both 1954 and 1956, three of the state's ten congressmen were Democrats, and some observers noted a possible trend toward a real two-party alignment within Wisconsin. The shift away from an exclusively Republican state was aided by the growing power of organized labor and some dissatisfaction with President Eisenhower's farm policies. The election of Democrat Gaylord Nelson as governor in 1958 underscored the trend. A diversity of economic interests and a combination of farm and city environment contributed to a more varied and less predictable political life for the Badger State.

The unpredictability and diversity continued to be in evidence in the election of 1960. In that presidential year Wisconsin voters cast 895,175 ballots for Richard M. Nixon, the Republican candidate, and 830,805 for the victorious John F. Kennedy. Within state politics Governor Gaylord Nelson was elected for a second term by a close vote. The attorney general was also a Democrat, but the Republicans elected their candidates for lieutenant governor, secretary of state, and treasurer. In the legislature Republicans remained in control of the state senate and recaptured control of the assembly. Whatever the future of Wisconsin politics might be, it was unlikely that either party would be able to take the voters for granted, but it was just as unlikely that any significant third party comparable to the Progressives would develop.

If the political future of Wisconsin was uncertain in 1960, so was the ultimate solution of other pressing problems faced by the people of the state. As in other parts of the nation, Wisconsin's crowded urban areas were plagued with exasperating rush-hour traffic jams and a shortage of parking space. The spiraling cost of goods, services, and government threatened more inflation and new taxes to pay for extended government services. Once again farmers' income failed to keep pace with the rising cost of dairying and other agricultural pursuits. And more and more Wisconsin citizens realized that some of their problems originated in other places. If there ever had been such a thing as Midwestern isolationism, few if any thinking people would cling to it in 1960. By then Wisconsin, which began its history as an outpost of Europe, had become an integral part of a strong nation which was literally the heart of the non-Communist world. Problems of international statecraft and even of survival itself in an atomic age profoundly disturbed Wisconsinites. Yet with Wisconsin's heritage of unusually intelligent use of its human and natural resources, few in the state would despair for its future—even in the rapidly changing, highly complex world of the mid-twentieth century.

SUGGESTED ADDITIONAL READING

Altmeyer, Arthur J. "The Wisconsin Idea and Social Security," in the *Wisconsin Magazine of History*, 42:19–25 (Autumn, 1958).

Austin, H. Russell. *The Wisconsin Story: The Building of a Vanguard State* (Milwaukee, 1957), 287–341.

Butts, Porter. *Art in Wisconsin* (Madison, 1936).

Clark, James I. *John Muir . . . Wanderer* (Madison, 1957).
————. *Wisconsin Meets the Great Depression* (Madison, 1956).
Carstensen, Vernon. *Farms or Forests: Evolution of a State Land Policy for Northern Wisconsin, 1850–1932* (Madison, 1958).
Doan, Edward N., *The La Follettes and the Wisconsin Idea* (New York, 1947).
Epstein, Leon D. *Politics in Wisconsin* (Madison, 1958).
Hoglund, A. William. "Wisconsin Dairy Farmers on Strike," in *Agricultural History*, 35:24–34 (January, 1961).
Holmes, Fred L. *Wisconsin* (5 vols., Chicago, 1946), II, 245–256, 500–512.
Jacobs, Herbert. "The Wisconsin Milk Strike," in the *Wisconsin Magazine of History*, 35:30–35 (Autumn, 1951).
Manson, Grant Carpenter. *Frank Lloyd Wright to 1910: The First Golden Age* (New York, 1958).
McCoy, Donald R. "The National Progressives of America," in the *Mississippi Valley Historical Review*, 44:75–93 (June, 1957).
Raney, William Francis. *Wisconsin: A Story of Progress* (New York, 1940), 399–421, 492–518.
Schorer, C. E. "Hamlin Garland of Wisconsin," in the *Wisconsin Magazine of History*, 37:147–150, 182–185 (Spring, 1954).
Still, Bayrd. *Milwaukee: The History of a City* (Madison, 1948), 497–514, 528–568.
Swift, Ernest. "The Conservation Department—Men and Machines at Work," in the *Wisconsin Magazine of History*, 37: 3–6, 48–50 (Autumn, 1953).
Wilson, F. G. "Zoning for Forestry and Recreation: Wisconsin's Pioneer Role," in the *Wisconsin Magazine of History*, 41:102–106 (Winter, 1957–1958).
"Wisconsin in 1958," in the *Wisconsin Blue Book* (Madison, 1958), 69–222.
Witte, Edwin E. "Some Trends Revealed by the 1940 Census," in the *Wisconsin Blue Book* (Madison, 1942), 129–150.
Wright, Frank Lloyd. *An Autobiography* (New York, 1943).

Index

Dodgeville, 40, 51, 56
Doolittle, James R., 88
Door County Fruit Growers
 Union, 187
Dorchester, 145
Doty, James Duane: 42, 48, 59,
 72, 75; and development of
 Madison, 49–50, 58; conflict
 with Dodge, 52–54
Douglas, Stephen A., 50, 102,
 106
Draper, Lyman C.: 83–84;
 quoted, 84–85; and State
 Historical Society, 86–87
Duluth, Daniel Greysolon,
 Sieur, 16
Duluth, Minnesota, 145
Durkee, Charles, 100–101

EAGLE REGIMENT, 110
Eau Claire, 164, 232, 237
Education: before 1862, 83–85;
 during Civil War, 124; 1876–
 1900, 162–165; since 1900,
 240–243
Eight-hour-day movement, 161–
 162, 221
Eighteenth Amendment, 216–
 217
Eisenhower, Dwight D., 269
Ekern, Herman L., 203, 204
Eleventh Story League, 207.
 See also Republican Party
Ely, Richard T., 175, 178
Engagés, 9. *See also* Fur trade
England: and Seven Years'
 War, 25–26; co-operatives in,
 186. *See also* British
English Prairie (Muscoda), 26
Episcopal Church, 65
Erin Prairie: described, 153
Espionage Act (federal), 212,
 223–224
Evjue, William T., 259

FAAST, BENJAMIN F., 189
Fairchild, Lucius, 109, 130
Farm Credit Association, 256
Farm Holiday, 255
Farm mortgages, 119–120
Farm tenancy, 186. *See also*
 Agriculture
Farwell, Leonard J., 131
Featherstonhaugh, George W.,
 48
Ferber, Edna, 243
Finnish immigrants, 186–187
Flour milling, 94
Fond du Lac, 109, 143
Fond du Lac County, 121
Forest crop law, 1927, 239–240
Fort Armstrong (Rock Island,
 Ill.), 43
Fort Crawford (Prairie du
 Chien), 41, 42
Fort Dearborn, 31
Fort Duquesne (Pittsburgh),
 25
Fort Edward Augustus (Green
 Bay), 26
Fort Howard (Green Bay), 41,
 42
Fort Shelby (Prairie du Chien),
 31
Fort Wayne, Ind., 40
Fort Winnebago (Portage), 41,
 42
Forty-Eighters, 91–93, 115–116
Four Lakes region, 46, 47
Fourier, Charles, 62
Fox Indians: 3, 4, 14, 26; wars
 of, 7, 23
Fox River, 2, 7, 14, 20, 63, 144
Fox-Wisconsin waterway, 59
France: importance of fur trade
 to, 7–11; and Seven Years'
 War, 25–26. *See also* French
Frank, Glenn, 260
Frank, Michael, 87–88
Franklin, Benjamin, 32

Higby, Lewis J., 132
Hoan, Daniel W., 223, 250
Hoard, William Dempster, 151
Hollyhock House, 246
Horicon, 50
Horlick, William, 166
Howe, Frederic C., 201
Howe, Timothy O., 88
Hubbell, Levi, 77–78
Hughitt, Marvin, 209
Hull, Cordell, 258
Huron Indians, 3, 6–7, 20
Husting, Paul Oscar, 208
Hutchins, Frank A., 201

ILLINOIS, 27, 28, 33, 72, 104, 172
Illinois Central Railroad, 106
Illinois Indians, 6, 21
Illinois-Michigan Canal, 95
Illinois Territory: Wisconsin a part of, 64
Immigrants: active in co-operative movement, 186–187; in cutover lands, 144; in Milwaukee, 159–161
Immigration: during territorial period, 60–61; 1848–1860, 89–93; in 1870's, 149; 1876–1900, 152–154, 159–161
Indiana: Rappites in, 61–62
Indiana Territory: 29; Wisconsin a part of, 64
Indians: 2–7; relations with French, 4–7, 11–16, 24–25, 28; relations with British, 7, 24, 26–29; described, 8, 13–14; and American Revolution, 28–29; relations with Americans, 29–30, 41–46, 112–113; treaties, 46, 139. See also Fur Trade; Missionaries; the several tribes
Industrial development: during Civil War, 121–122; 1876–

Industrial development (Continued)
1900, 143–144, 156–159; 1900–1924, 184, 188; since 1924, 237–238, 263–264
Internal improvements, 59–60, 74, 104–107, 130
Inventors, 165–169
Iowa: part of Wisconsin Territory, 58, 64
Irish immigrants, 153, 154
Iron Brigade, 109–110
Iroquois Indians, 3, 6–7, 13, 14, 20
Italian immigrants: in Milwaukee, 160

JACKSON, ANDREW, 51
Jacksonians, 64–65. See also Democratic Party
James, Ada L., 217
Janesville, 263
Jastrow, Joseph, 175
Jay's Treaty, 29, 32
Jefferson County, 152
Jesuits, 4, 5, 17–23
Jewish immigrants: in Milwaukee, 160
Johns Hopkins University, 175
Jolliet, Louis, 22
Jones, George Wallace, 48
Junction City, 145
Juneau, Solomon, 57–58

KALAMAZOO, MICHIGAN, 163
Kansas, 149
Kansas-Nebraska Bill, 102
Keep, Albert, 148
Kennedy, John F., 269
Keyes, Elisha W., 126, 130, 170, 174
Kenosha: 88, 232; public schools, 83; development of, 237; defense industries in, 263

278 / Index

Leather industry, 121
Legislative Reference Library, 200, 201
Lenroot, Irvine L., 203, 204, 207–208
Leonard, William Ellery, 201, 245
Liberty Party, 100
Life magazine, 258
Lighty, William H., 200
Lilienthal, David, 252
Lincoln, Abraham: 50, 104, 126; opposition to, 115–117
Live Stock Sanitary Board, 185
Liverpool, England, 157
London, England, 27
Loomis, Orland S., 260
Louis XIV, of France, 22
Louisiana: 24; ceded to Spain, 26; Civil War battles in, 110
Louvigny, Louis de la Porte de, 23
Ludington, Michigan, 156
Lumbering: before 1860, 94; during Civil War, 121; 1876–1900, 138–143
Lutheran Church, 65, 89, 165

MACARTHUR, GEN. DOUGLAS, 261, 266
Mackinac, trading post, 24, 29, 31, 33
Madison: 55, 232; capital located at, 50, 58; constitutional conventions at, 74–77; public schools in, 83; Confederate prisoners at, 109; development since 1924, 235; *Argus,* 76; *Capital Times,* 259
Madison Club, 212
Madison Regency, 126, 130
Manila, battle of, 157
Manitowoc, 40, 121, 264
Marietta, Ohio, 40

Marquette, Father Jacques, 21, 22
Marquette University, 165
Marshfield, 145
Martin, Morgan L., 58, 59
Mascoutin Indians, 3, 7
Maumee River, 40
McCarthy, Charles, 200, 201, 204, 212; *The Wisconsin Idea,* 201
McCarthy, Joseph R., 258, 268–269
McGovern, Francis E., 203–204, 207–208
Meat packing, 121
Memphis, Tenn., 114
Ménard, Father Rene, 17, 19–20
Menasha, 143, 145
Menominee Indians, 3, 7, 14, 26
Menominee River, 7
Merrill, 144
Methodist Church, 65, 165
Mexican War, 43
Meyer, C. J. L., 143
Miami Indians, 21, 24
Michigan: 63, 172; Indians in, 21; early settlement, 40; supreme court, 163
Michigan Territory: Wisconsin a part of, 64
Migrant farm workers, 232
Military rule in Wisconsin, 41–43
Milk strikes, 255–256
Milk tester, invention of, 166–167
Milton College, 165
Milwaukee: 55, 106, 109, 196; early settlement, 40, 58, 59; as lake port, 60, 118, 238; Germans in, 61, 92–93, 159–161; public schools in, 83; Democrats in, 116–117, 127–128; industrial development,

Northwestern Packet Company, 118
Norwegian immigrants, 61, 203
Nova Scotia, 33
Nye, Gerald P., 260

OCONTO RIVER, 4
Ohio, 47, 50, 62
Ohio Valley, 32
Oil boom, 1865, 123
Old Briton, Miami chief, 24–25
Ontario, 19
Oregon, 50
Oshkosh, 143, 164, 169, 170
Ottawa Indians, 3, 6, 13, 19–20, 46
Otto, Max C.: quoted, 206
Owen, John: quoted, 60
Owen, Robert, 62
Ozaukee County, 116

PABST, FREDERICK, 160
Pabst breweries, 157
Panic: of 1837, 59, 69; of 1857, 80–81, 82, 95–96, 118, 123; of 1873, 147; of 1893, 173
Paper making, 143–144
Paris, France: 9, 27; exposition of 1900, 167
Payne, Henry C., 191
Pearl Harbor, attack on, 263
Peary, Admiral Robert E., 157
Peat mining, 123
Pecatonica River, 46
Peck, George W., 172, 259
Pennsylvania, 62
Pennsylvania State College, 200
People's Party, 221
Perrot, Nicolas: 13–14; quoted, 15–16
Peshtigo, 141
Pfister and Vogel, Milwaukee firm, 157

Philadelphia: 24, 32; Centennial Exhibition of 1876, 151
Philipp, Gov. Emanuel L., 211, 217
Pickawillany, trading post, 24
Piqua, Ohio, 24
Pittsburgh, Pennsylvania, 157
Plains of Abraham, battle of, 25
Plank roads, 59
Plankinton House, Milwaukee, 196
Platteville, 40, 55, 164
Polish immigrants, 154, 160
Polk, James K., 74
Pomeroy, Marcus M., 117
Pontiac, Ottawa chief, 26
Populist Party, 221
Port Edwards, 144
Portage, 41, 42
Portage County, 154
Potawatomi Indians, 3, 4, 7, 13, 20, 46
Potter Law, 1873, 147–148
Prairie du Chien: 40, 46; Fort Shelby at, 31; Fort Crawford at, 41, 42; Indian Council at, 43; railroad reached, 80
Presbyterian Church, 65, 165
Primary election law, 1903, 199, 205
Proclamation Line, 26–27, 32
Progressive magazine, 259
Progressive movement: beginnings, 174, 180, 183–184, 191–192; 1900–1905, 196–199; achievements, 200–204; factions within, 202–208; and World War I, 210–211; 1920–1924, 217–221; campaign of 1924, 219–220; 1925–1946, 229, 257–262
Progressive Party: 1912, 210; 1936, 259–260
Prohibition, 216–217

WABASH RIVER, 27, 40
Wahl, Christian, 160
Walker, George H., 58
Walworth County, 152
War of 1812, 1, 29–31
Washburn, Cadwallader C., 56–57, 82, 88, 110, 132
Washington County, 116
Watertown, 165
Waukesha, 85
Wausau, 144
Wells, Oliver E., 178
Weyerhaeuser, Frederick, 142–143
WHA, radio station, 242
Wheat, importance of, 93–94, 118–119, 120, 149
Wheeler, Burton K., 219–220, 260
Wheeling, West Virginia, 268
Whigs, 64–65, 75, 100
Whitewater, 164
Whiton, Edward V., 88
Wildcat money, 81–82
Williams College, 174
Williamsburg, battle of, 110
Wilson, Woodrow, 211, 218
Winnebago Indians, 3, 4, 6, 11, 14, 26, 30, 46, 54
Wisconsin: French occupation, 1–26 *passim;* origin of name, 2; physical description, 2; British occupation, 26–28; territorial status, 38–66 *passim,* 71; statehood achieved, 68–77; during Civil War, 99–100, 106–118; in Spanish-American War, 170; in World War I, 208, 210–216; in World War II, 261, 262–266
Wisconsin Agricultural Authority, 254
Wisconsin Bank of Mineral Point, 56

Wisconsin Bankers Association, 123
Wisconsin Central Railroad, 145
Wisconsin Cooperative Milk Pool, 255
Wisconsin Dairymen's Association, 151, 152
Wisconsin Development Authority, 254
Wisconsin Farm and Credit Association, 256
Wisconsin Free Library Commission, 201
Wisconsin Grange, 147
Wisconsin Idea, 175, 200, 214, 216, 218, 225, 251–252. *See also* Progressive movement
Wisconsin Industrial Commission, 200, 202, 252
Wisconsin Players, 243
Wisconsin River: 2, 46; lumbering on, 138; paper industry on, 144
Wisconsin Society of Equity, 204
Wisconsin State Council of Defense, 214
Wisconsin State Senate, 212
Wisconsin Supreme Court: nullified Fugitive Slave Law, 103–104; upheld Potter Law, 148
Witte, Edwin E., 251
Wolf River, 138
Woman Suffrage Association, 217
Woodman, Cyrus, 55–57, 82
World Court, 258
World War I: 210–216; opposed by La Follette, 208
World War II, 258, 261, 262–266
W.P.A., 252, 253